Margaret Cavendish

The Life of the thrice, noble, high and puissant Prince William Cavendish, Duke, Marquess and Earl of Newcastle

Margaret Cavendish

The Life of the thrice, noble, high and puissant Prince William Cavendish, Duke, Marquess and Earl of Newcastle

ISBN/EAN: 9783742802293

Manufactured in Europe, USA, Canada, Australia, Japa

Cover: Foto ©Thomas Meinert / pixelio.de

Manufactured and distributed by brebook publishing software (www.brebook.com)

Margaret Cavendish

The Life of the thrice, noble, high and puissant Prince William Cavendish, Duke, Marquess and Earl of Newcastle

Thus in this Semy-Circle wher they Sitt,
Telling of Tales of pleasure & of witt.
Heer you may read without a Sinn or Crime,
And how more innocently pass your tyme.

The Duke and Dutchess of Newcastle and their Family.

THE
LIFE
OF THE
Thrice Noble, High and Puissant PRINCE
William Cavendishe,

Duke, Marquess, and Earl of *Newcastle*; Earl
of *Ogle*; Viscount *Mansfield*; and Baron of
Bolsover, of *Ogle*, *Bothal* and *Hepple*: Gentle-
man of His Majesties Bed-chamber; one of His
Majesties most Honourable Privy-Councel;
Knight of the most Noble Order of the Garter;
His Majesties Lieutenant of the County and
Town of *Nottingham*; and Justice in Ayre
Trent-North: who had the honour to be Gover-
nour to our most Glorious King, and Gracious
Soveraign, in his Youth, when He was Prince
of *Wales*; and soon after was made Captain Ge-
neral of all the Provinces beyond the River of
Trent, and other Parts of the Kingdom of *Eng-
land*, with Power, by a special Commission, to
make Knights.

WRITTEN
By the thrice Noble, Illustrious, and Excellent Princess,
MARGARET, *Duchess of* Newcastle,
His Wife.

LONDON,
Printed by *A. Maxwell*, in the Year 1667.

CHAPTERS SIX

Charles the Second

... and his ... reign of ...

... Marginal Note

I have, in confidence of your Goodness, ... behalfe, or rather the general ... of our Marche ... situation ... ... or ... you to ... of the Report, and sufferings of your ... Lord ... Smock ... and Husband say Your ... ... the ... viewing, who ... Your Majesties Favour, ... was Yeomon ... of the ... ... and ... for ... ... I have heard him ...

To His moſt Sacred

MAJESTY

Charles the Second,

By the Grace of God, of *England, Scotland, France*
and *Ireland* King, Defender of the Faith,*&c.*

May it pleaſe Your Majeſty,

I Have, in confidence of your Gracious acceptance, taken the boldneſs, or rather the
preſumption, to dedicate to Your Majeſty
this ſhort Hiſtory (which is as full of Truths,as words)
of the Actions and Sufferings of Your moſt Loyal
Subject, my Lord and Husband (by Your Majeſties late favour) Duke of *Newcaſtle*; who when Your
Majeſty was Prince of *Wales,* was Your moſt careful
Governour, and honeſt Servant. Give me therefore leave to relate here, that I have heard him often
ſay,

say, He loves Your Royal Perſon ſo dearly, that He would moſt willingly, upon all occaſions, ſacrifice his Life and Poſterity for Your Majeſty : whom that Heaven will ever bleſs, is the Prayer of

Your moſt Obedient, Loyal,

humble Subject

and Servant,

Margaret Newcaſtle.

TO

TO HIS
GRACE
THE
Duke of Newcastle.

My Noble Lord,

IT hath always been my hearty Prayer to God, since I have been your Wife, That first I might prove an honest and good Wife, whereof your Grace must be the onely Judg: Next, That God would be pleased to enable me to set forth and declare to after-ages, the truth of your loyal actions and endeavours, for the service of your King and Country; For the accomplishing of which design, I have followed the best and truest Observations of your Secretary John Rolleston, and your Lordships own Relations, and have accordingly writ the History of your Lordships Life, which although I have endeavoured to render as perspicuous as ever I could, yet one thing I find hath much darkned it;

which

which is, that your Grace commanded me not to mention
any thing or passage to the prejudice or disgrace of any Family or particular person (although they might be of great
truth, and would illustrate much the actions of your Life)
which I have dutifully performed to satisfie your Lordship,
whose Nature is so Generous, that you are as well pleased to obscure the faults of your Enemies, as you are to divulge the
vertues of your Friends; And certainly, My Lord, you have
had as many Enemies, and as many Friends, as ever any one
particular person had; and I pray God to forgive the one,
and prosper the other: Nor do I so much wonder at it, since
I, a Woman, cannot be exempt from the malice and aspersions of spightful tongues, which they cast upon my poor
Writings, some denying me to be the true Authoress of
them; for your Grace remembers well, that those Books
I put out first, to the judgment of this censorious Age, were
accounted not to be written by a Woman, but that some body
else had writ and publish'd them in my Name; by which
your Lordship was moved to prefix an Epistle before one of
them in my vindication, wherein you assure the world upon
your honour, That what was written and printed in my
name, was my own; and I have also made known, that your
Lordship was my onely Tutor, in declaring to me what you
had found and observed by your own experience; for I being
young when your Lordship married me, could not have much
knowledg of the world; But it pleased God to command his
Servant Nature to indue me with a Poetical and Philosophical Genius, even from my Birth; for I did write some

Books

Books in that kind, before I was twelve years of Age, which for want of good method and order, I would never divulge. But though the world would not believe that those Conceptions and Fancies which I writ, were my own, but transcended my capacity, yet they found fault, that they were defective for want of Learning; and on the other side, they said I had pluckt Feathers out of the Universities; which was a very preposterous judgment. Truly My Lord, I confess that for want of Scholarship, I could not express my self so well as otherwise I might have done, in those Philosophical Writings I publish'd first; but after I was returned with your Lordship into my Native Country, and led a retired Country life, I applied my self to the reading of Philosophical Authors, of purpose to learn those names and words of Art that are used in Schools; which at first were so hard to me, that I could not understand them, but was fain to guess at the sense of them by the whole context, and so writ them down as I found them in those Authors, at which my Readers did wonder, and thought it impossible that a Woman could have so much Learning and Understanding in Terms of Art, and Scholastical Expressions; so that I and my Books are like the old Apologue mention'd in Æsop, of a Father, and his Son, who rid on an Ass through a Town when his Father went on Foot, at which sight the People shouted and cried shame, that a young Boy should ride, and let his Father, an old man, go on Foot: whereupon the old Man got upon the Ass, and let his Son go by; but when they came to the next Town, the People exclaimed

exclaimed against the Father, that he a lusty man should ride, and have no more pity of his young and tender child, but let him go on foot: Then both the Father and his Son got upon the Ass, and coming to the third Town, the People blamed them both for being so unconscionable as to over-burden the poor Ass with their heavy weight: After this both Father and Son went on foot, and led the Ass; and when they came to the fourth Town, the People railed as much at them as ever the former had done, and called them both Fools, for going on foot, when they had a Beast able to carry them. The old Man, seeing he could not please Mankind in any manner, and having received so many blemishes and aspersions, for the sake of his Ass, was at last resolved to drown him when he came to the next bridg. But I am not so passionate to burn my Writings for the various humours of Mankind, and for their finding fault, since there is nothing in this world, be it the noblest and most commendable action whatsoever, that shall escape blameless. As for my being the true and onely Authoress of them, your Lordship knows best, and my attending Servants are witness that I have had none but my own Thoughts, Fancies and Speculations to assist me; and as soon as I have set them down, I send them to those that are to transcribe them, and fit them for the Press; whereof since there have been several, and amongst them such as onely could write a good hand, but neither understood Orthography, nor had any Learning (I being then in banishment with your Lordship, and not able to maintain learned Secretaries) which hath been a great

dis-

disadvantage to my poor works, and the cause that they have been printed so false, and so full of Errors; for besides that, I want also the skill of Scholarship and true writing, I did many times not peruse the Copies that were transcribed, lest they should disturb my following Conceptions; by which neglect, as I said, many Errors are slipt into my Works, which yet I hope Learned and Impartial Readers will soon rectifie, and look more upon the sense, then carp at words. I have been a Student even from my Childhood; and since I have been your Lordships Wife, I have lived for the most part a strict and retired Life, as is best known to your Lordship, and therefore my Censurers cannot know much of me, since they have little or no acquaintance with me: 'Tis true, I have been a Traveller both before and after I was married to your Lordship, aud sometimes shew my self at your Lordships Command in Publick places or Assemblies; but yet I converse with few. Indeed, My Lord, I matter not the Censures of this Age, but am rather proud of them; for it shews that my Actions are more then ordinary, and according to the old Proverb, It is better to be Envied, then Pitied: for I know well, that it is meerly out of spight and malice, whereof this present Age is so full, that none can escape them, and they'l make no doubt to stain even Your Lordships Loyal, Noble and Heroick Actions, as well as they do mine, though yours have been of War and Fighting, mine of Contemplating and Writing: Yours were performed publickly in the Field, mine privately in my Closet: Yours had many thousand Eye-witnesses, mine none

but

but my Waiting-maids. But the Great God that hath hitherto bless'd both Your Grace and me, will, I question not, preserve both our Fames to after Ages, for which we shall be bound most humbly to acknowledg his great Mercy; and I my self, as long as I live, be

Your Graces Honest Wife,

and Humble Servant

M. NEWCASTLE.

THE

THE
PREFACE.

WHen I firſt Intended to write this Hiſtory, knowing my ſelf to be no Scholar, and as ignorant of the Rules of writing Hiſtories, as I have in my other Works acknowledg'd my ſelf to be of the Names and Terms of Art ; I deſired my Lord, That he would be pleaſed to let me have ſome Elegant and Learned Hiſtorian to aſſiſt me; which requeſt his Grace would not grant me ; ſaying, That having never had any Aſſiſtance in the writing of my former Books, I ſhould have no other in the writing of his Life, but the Informations from himſelf, and his Secretary, of the chief Tranſactions and Fortunes occurring in it, to the time he married me. I humbly anſwer'd, That without a learned Aſſiſtant, the Hiſtory would be defective: But he replied, That Truth could not be defective. I ſaid again, That

Rhetorick

Rhetorick did adorn Truth : And he anſwer'd, That Rhetorick was fitter for Falſhoods then Truths. Thus I was forced by his Graces Commands, to write this Hiſtory in my own plain Style, without elegant Flouriſhings, or exquiſit Method, relying intirely upon Truth, in the expreſſing whereof, I have been very circumſpect ; as knowing well, that his Graces Actions have ſo much Glory of their own, that they need borrow none from any bodies Induſtry.

Many Learned Men, I know, have publiſhed Rules and Directions concerning the Method and Style of Hiſtories, and do with great noiſe, to little purpoſe, make loud exclamations againſt thoſe Hiſtorians, that keeping cloſe to the Truth of their Narrations, cannot think it neceſſary to follow ſlaviſhly ſuch Inſtructions ; and there is ſome Men of good Underſtandings, as I have heard, that applaud very much ſeveral Hiſtories, meerly for their Elegant Style, and well-obſerv'd Method ; ſetting a high value upon feigned Orations, myſtical Deſigns, and fancied Policies, which are, at the beſt, but pleaſant Romances. Others approve, in the Relations of Wars, and of Military Actions, ſuch tedious Deſcriptions, that the Reader, tired with them, will imagine that there was more time ſpent in Aſſaulting, Defending, and taking of a Fort, or a petty Gariſon, then *Alexander* did employ in conquering the greateſt part of the World; which proves, That ſuch Hiſtorians regard more their

own

own Eloquence, Wit and Industry, and the knowledg they believe to have of the Actions of War, and of all manner of Governments, than of the truth of the History, which is the main thing, and wherein consists the hardest task, very few Historians knowing the Transactions they write of, and much less the Counsels, and secret Designs of many different Parties, which they confidently mention.

Although there be many sorts of Histories, yet these three are the chiefest: 1. a General History. 2. A National History. 3. A Particular History. Which three sorts may, not unfitly, be compared to the three sorts of Governments, Democracy, Aristocracy, and Monarchy. The first is the History of the known parts and people of the World; The second is the History of a particular Nation, Kingdom or Commonwealth. The third is the History of the life and actions of some particular Person. The first is profitable for Travellers, Navigators and Merchants; the second is pernicious, by reason it teaches subtil Policies, begets Factions, not onely between particular Families and Persons, but also between whole Nations, and great Princes, rubbing old sores, and renewing old Quarrels, that would otherwise have been forgotten. The last is the most secure; because it goes not out of its own Circle, but turns on its own Axis, and for the most part, keeps within the Circumference of Truth. The first is Mechanical, the second

(c)   Political,

Political, and the third Heroical. The first should onely be written by Travellers, and Navigators; The second by Statesmen; The third by the Prime Actors, or the Spectators of those Affairs and Actions of which they write, as *Cæsars* Commentaries are, which no Pen but of such an Author, who was also Actor in the particular Occurrences, private Intrigues, secret Counsels, close Designs, and rare Exploits of War he relates, could ever have brought to so high Perfection.

This History is of the Third sort, as that is; and being of the Life and Actions of my Noble Lord and Husband, who hath informed me of all the particular passages I have recorded, I cannot, though neither Actor, nor Spectator, be thought ignorant of the Truth of what I write; Nor is it inconsistent with my being a Woman, to write of Wars, that was neither between *Medes* and *Persians*, *Greeks* and *Trojans*, *Christians* and *Turks*; but among my own Countreymen, whose Customs and Inclinations, and most of the Persons that held any considerable Place in the Armies, was well known to me; and besides all that (which is above all) my Noble and Loyal Lord did act a chief Part in that fatal Tragedy, to have defended (if humane power could have done it) his most Gracious Soveraign, from the fury of his Rebellious Subjects.

This

This History being (as I have said) of a particular Person, his Actions, and Fortunes; it cannot be expected, that I should here Preach of the beginning of the World; nor seem to express understanding in the Politicks, by tedious moral Discourses, with long Observations upon the several sorts of Government that have been in *Greece* & *Rome*, and upon others more modern; I will neither endeavour to make show of Eloquence, making Speeches that never was spoken, nor pretend to great skill in War, by making Mountains of Mole-hills, and telling Romansical Falshoods for Historical Truths; and much less will I write to amuse my Readers, in a mystical and allegorical Style, of the disloyal Actions of the opposite Party, of the Treacherous Cowardise, Envy and Malice of some Persons, my Lords Enemies, and of the ingratitude of some of his seeming Friends; wherein I cannot better obey his Lordships Commands to conceal those things, then in leaving them quite out, as I do, with submission to his Lordships desire, from whom I have learn'd Patience to overcome my Passions, and Discretion to yield to his Prudence.

Thus am I resolved to write, in a natural plain style, without Latin Sentences, moral Instructions, politick Designs, feigned Orations, or envious and malicious Exclamations, this short History of the Loyal, Heroick and Prudent Actions of my Noble Lord, as also of his Sufferings, Losses, and ill-Fortunes,
which

which in honour and Confcience I could not fuffer to be buried in filence; nor could I have undertaken fo hard a task, had not my love to his Perfon, and to Truth, been my Encourager and Supporter.

I might have made this Book larger, in tranfcribing (as is ordinary in Hiftories) the feveral Letters, full of Affection, and kind promifes he received from His Gracious Soveraign, *Charles* the Firft, and from his Royal Confort, in the time he was in the Actions of War, as alfo fince the War, from his dear Soveraign and Mafter, *Charles* the Second; But many of the former Letters having been loft, when all was loft; I thought it beft, feeing I had not them all, to print none. As for Orations, which is another way of fwelling the bulk of Hiftories; it is certain, that My Lord made not many; chufing rather to fight, then to talk; and his Declarations having been printed already, it had been fuperfluous to infert them in thefe Narrations.

This Book would however, have been a great Volume, if his Grace would have given me leave to publifh his Enemies Actions; But being to write of his own onely, I do it briefly and truly; and not as many have done, who have written of the late Civil War, with but few fprinklings of Truth, like as Heat-drops upon a dry barren Ground; knowing no more of the Tranfactions of thofe Times, then what they learned in the Gazets, which, for the moft part, (out of Policy

licy to amufe and deceive the People) contain nothing
but Falfhoods and Chimeraes; and were fuch Para-
fites, that after the Kings Party was over-powred,
the Government among the Rebels changing from
one Faction to another, they never mifs'd to exalt
highly the Merits of the chief Commanders of the then
prevailing fide, comparing fome of them to *Mofes*,
and fome others to all the great and moft famous He-
roes, both Greeks and Romans; wherein, unawares,
they exceedingly commended my Noble Lord; for
if thofe Ring-leaders of Factions were fo great men as
they are reported to be, by thofe Time-fervers, How
much greater muft his Lordfhip be, who beat moft of
them, except the Earl of *Effex*, whofe employment
was never in the Northern parts, where all the reft of
the greateft ftrength of the Parliament was fent, to oppofe my Lord's Forces, which was the greateft the
Kings Party had any where.

Good Fortune is fuch an Idol of the World, and
is fo like the golden Calf worfhipped by the Ifra-
elites, that thofe Arch-Rebels never wanted Aftro-
logers to foretel them good fuccefs in all their Enter-
prifes, nor Poets to fing their Praifes, nor Orators for
Panegyricks; nay, which is worfe, nor Hiftorians
neither, to record their Valour in fighting, and Wifdom in Governing. But being, fo much as I am, a-
bove bafe Profit, or any Preferment whatfoever, I
cannot fear to be fufpected of Flattery, in declaring

(d)   to to the World the Merits, Wealth, Power, Loyalty, and Fortunes of My Noble Lord, who hath done great Actions, suffered great Losses, endured a long Banishment, for his Loyalty to his King and Countrey ; and leads now, like another *Scipio*, a quiet Countrey-life. If notwithstanding all this, any should say, That those who write Histories of themselves, and their own actions, or of their own Party, or instruct and inform those that write them, are partial to themselves ; I answer, That it is very improbable, Worthy Persons, who having done Great, Noble and Heroick Exploits, deserving to be recorded, should be so vain, as to write false Histories ; but if they do, it proves but their Folly ; for Truth can never be concealed, and so it will be more for their disgrace, then for their Honour or Fame. I fear not any such blemishes in this present History, for I am conscious of any such Crime as Patiality or Falshood, but write it whilest My Noble Lord is yet alive, and at such a time where Truth may be declared, and Falshood contradicted ; and I challenge any one (although I be a Woman) to contradict any thing that I have set down, or prove it to be otherwise then Truth ; for be there never so many Contradictions, Truth will conquer all at last.

Concerning My Lords Actions in War, which are comprehended in the first Book, the relation of them I have chiefly from my Lords Secretary Mr. *Rolleston*, a Person that has been an Eye-witness thereof, and

ac-

accompanied My Lord as Secretary in his Army, and gave out all his Commiſſions ; his honeſty and worth is unqueſtionable by all that know him. And as for the Second Book, which contains My Lords Actions and Sufferings, during the time of his Exile, I have ſet down ſo much as I could poſſibly call to mind, without any particular Expreſſion of time, onely from the time of his Baniſhment, or rather (what I can remember) from the time of my Marriage, till our return into *England.* To the end of which I have joined a Computation of My Lord's Loſſes, which he hath ſuffered by thoſe unfortunate Warres. In the third Book I have ſet down ſome particular Chapters concerning the Deſcription of his Perſon, his Natural Faculties, and Perſonal Vertues, *&c.* And in the laſt, ſome Eſſayes and Diſcourſes of My Lords, together with ſome Notes and Remarques of mine own; which I thought moſt convenient to place by themſelves at the end of this Work, rather then to intermingle them with the Body of the Hiſtory.

It might be ſome prejudice to my Lord's Glory, and the credit of this Hiſtory, not to take notice of a very conſiderable thing I have heard, which is, That when his Lordſhip's Army had got ſo much Strength and Reputation, that the Rebellious Parliament finding themſelves overpower'd with it, rather then to be utterly ruin'd, (as was unavoidable) did call the *Scots* to their Aſſiſtance, with a promiſe to reward ſo

great

great a Service, with the Four Northern Counties of *Northumberland*, *Cumberland*, *Westmerland*, and the Bishoprick of *Durham*, which I have not mention'd in the Book.

And it is most certain, That the Parliaments Forces were never Powerful, nor their Commanders or Officers Famous, until such time as my Lord was overpower'd; neither could Loyalty have been overpower'd by Rebellion, had not Treachery had better Fortune then Prudence.

When I speak of my Lord's Pedigree, where *Thomas* Earl of *Arundel*, Grandfather to the now Duke of *Norfolk*, is mention'd, they have left out *William* Viscount *Stafford*, one of his Sons, who did marry the Heir of the last Baron *Stafford*, descended from the Dukes of *Buckingham*; which was set down in my Original Manuscript.

Some of those Omissions, and very probably others, are happened, partly for want of timely Information, and chiefly by the death of my Secretary, who did copy my Writings for the Press, and dy'd in *London*, attending that Service, afore the Printing of the Book was quite finish'd. And as I hope of your Favour to be excus'd for omitting those things in the Book; so I expect of your Justice to be approv'd in putting them here, though somewhat unseasonably.

Before I end this Preface, I do beseech my Readers not to mistake me when I speak of my Lord's Banishment,

ment, as if I would conceal that he went voluntarily
out of his Native Country; for it is moſt true, that his
Lordſhip prudently perceiving all the King's Party
loſt, not onely in *England*, but alſo in *Scotland* and
Ireland; and that it was impoſſible to withſtand the
Rebels, after the fatal overthrow of his Army; his
Lordſhip, in a poor and mean condition quitted his
own Countrey, and went beyond Sea; ſoon after
which, the Rebels having got an Abſolute Power, and
granted a general Pardon to all thoſe that would come
in to them, upon compoſition, at the Rates they had ſet
down, his Lordſhip, with but few others, was excepted from it, both for Life and Eſtate, and did remain
thus baniſh'd till His Majeſties happy Reſtauration.

I muſt alſo acknowledg, That I have committed
great Errors in taking no notice of Times as I ſhould
have done in many places of this Hiſtory: I mention
in one place the Queen Mothers being in *France*, when
my Lord went thither, but do not ſay in what year
that was: Nor do I expreſs when His Majeſty (our
now Gracious Soveraign) came in, and went out a-
gain ſeveral times from that Kingdom, which has happen'd for want of Memory, and I deſire my Readers
to excuſe me for it.

No body can certainly be more ready to find faults
in this Work, then I am to confeſs them; being very
conſcious that I have, as I told my Lord I ſhould,
committed many for want of Learning, and chiefly
of

of skill in writing Histories: But having, according to his Lordships Commands, written his Actions and Fortunes truly and plainly, I have reason to expect, that whatsoever else shall be found amiss, will be favourably pardoned by the candid Readers, to whom I wish all manner of happiness.

AN

AN
EPISTLE
TO HER
GRACE
THE
Duchess of Newcastle.

May it please your Grace,

I *Have been taught, and do believe, That Obedience is better then Sacrifice; and know, that both are due from me to your Grace; and since I have been so long in obeying your Commands, I shall not presume to use any Arguments for my excuse, but rather chuse ingeniously to confess my fault, and beg your Graces Pardon. And because forgiveness is a Glory to the supreamest Powers, I will hope that your Grace by that great example will make it yours. And now*

(e)   I

I humbly take leave to represent to your Grace, as faithfully and truly as my memory will serve me, all my Observations of the most memorable Actions, and honourable Deportments of His Grace, my most Noble Lord and Master, William Duke of Newcastle, in the Execution and Performance of the Trusts and high Employments committed and commended to his care and charge by three Kings of England; that is to say, King James, King Charles the First, of ever blessed Memory; and our Gracious King, Charles the Second; under whom he hath had the happiness to live, and the honour to serve them in several capacities: And because I humbly conceive, that it is not within the intention of your Graces Commands, that I should give you a particular Relation of His Graces High Birth, his Noble and Princely Education and Breeding, both at home and abroad; his Natural Faculties, and Personal Vertues; his Justice, Bounty, Charity, Friendship; his Right Approved Courage, and True Valour, not grounded upon, or govern'd by Passion, but Reason; his Magnificent manner of living and supporting his Dignity, testified by his great Entertainments of their Majesties, and his private Friends, upon all fit occasions, besides his ordinary and constant House-keeping and Attendants; some for Honour, and some for business, wherein he exceeded most of his Quality; and that he was, and is an incomparable Master to his Servants, is sufficiently testified by all or most of the chiefest of them, living and dying in His Graces Service, which is an Argument that they thought themselves as

happy

happy therein, as the World could make them ; nor of his well-chosen Pleasures, which were principally Horses of all sorts , but more particularly Horses of Mannage ; His Study and Art of the true use of the Sword; His Magnificent Buidings. These are his chiefest Delights, wherein his Grace spared for no cost nor charge, which are sufficiently manifested to the World; for other Delights, as those of running Horses, Hawking, Hunting, &c. His Grace used them meerly for societies sake, and out of a generous and obliging Nature to please others, though his knowledg in them excelled, as well as in the other. And yet notwithstanding these his large and vast expences, before his Grace was called to the Court, he encreased his Revenue by way of Purchase to a great value ; and when he was called to the Court, he was then free from Debts, and, as I have heard, some Thousands of Pounds in his Purse. These Particulars, and as many more of this kind as would swell a Volume, I could enumerate to your Grace ; but that they are so well known to your Grace; it would be a Presumption in me, rather then a Service, to give your Grace that trouble ; and therefore I humbly forbear, and proceed, according to my Intention, to give your Grace a faithful account of Your Graces Commands, as becomes

May it please your Grace,

Your Graces most humble,

and most obedient Servant,

John Rolleston.

THE

THE
LIFE

OF THE

MOST ILLUSTRIOUS PRINCE,

WILLIAM
Duke of Newcastle.

The First Book.

Since my chief intent in this present Work, is to describe the Life and Actions of My Noble Lord and Husband, *William, Duke of Newcastle*, I shall do it with as much Brevity, Perspicuity and Truth, as is required of an Impartial Historian. The History of his Pedigree I shall refer to the Heralds, and partly give you an account thereof at the latter end of this work ; onely thus much I shall now mention, as will be requisite for the better understanding of the following discourse.

B   His

His Grandfather by his Fathers fide was Sir *William Cavendifh*, Privy Counsellour and Treafurer of the Chamber to King *Henry* the Eighth, *Edward* the Sixth, and Queen *Mary*. His Grandfather by his Mother was *Cuthbert* Lord *Ogle*, an ancient Baron. His Father Sir *Charles Cavendifh* was the youngeft fon to Sir *William*, and had no other Children but three Sons, whereof My Lord was the Second; but his elder Brother dying in his Infancy, left both his Title and Birth-right to My Lord, fo that My Lord had then but one onely Brother left, whofe name was *Charles* after his Father, whereas My Lord had the name of his Grandfather.

These two Brothers were partly bred with *Gilbert* Earl of *Shrewsbury* their Uncle in Law, and their Aunt *Mary*, Countefs of *Shrewsbury*, *Gilbert's* Wife, and Sifter to their Father; for there interceded an intire and conftant Friendfhip between the faid *Gilbert*, Earl of *Shrewsbury*, and My Lord's Father, Sir *Charles Cavendifh*, caufed not onely by the marriage of My Lord's Aunt, his Fathers Sifter, to the aforefaid *Gilbert* Earl of *Shrewsbury*, and by the marriage of *George* Earl of *Shrewsbury*, *Gilbert's* Father, with My Lord's Grandmother, by his Fathers fide; but Sir *Charles Cavendifh*, My Lord's Father, and *Gilbert* Earl of *Shrewsbury*, being brought up and bred together in one Family, and grown up as parts of one body, after they came to be beyond Children, and travelled together

ther

ther into foreign Countries, to obferve the Fafhions,
Laws, and Cuftoms of other Nations, contracted fuch
an intire Friendfhip which lafted to their death : neither
did they out-live each other long, for My Lord's Father, Sir *Charles Cavendifh,*lived but one year after *Gilbert* Earl of *Shrewsbury.*

But both My Lords Parents, and his Aunt and Uncle in Law, fhewed always a great and fond love to
My Lord, endeavouring, when He was but a Child,
to pleafe him with what he moft delighted in.   When
He was grown to the Age of fifteen or fixteen, he was
made Knight of the *Bath,* an ancient and honourable Order, at the time when *Henry,* King *James,* of
bleffed Memory, His eldeft Son was created Prince of
Wales : and foon after, he went to travel with Sir *Henry Wotton,* who was fent as Ambaffador Extraordinary to the then *Duke* of *Savoy;* which Duke made very
much of My Lord, and when he would be free in
Feafting, placed Him next to himfelf.   Before
My Lord did return with the Ambaffador into *England,* the faid Duke profer'd My Lord, that if he
would ftay with him, he would not onely confer upon him the beft Titles of Honour he could, but alfo
give him an honourable Command in War, although
My Lord was but young, for the Duke had then
fome defigns of War.   But the Ambaffador, who had
taken the care of My Lord, would not leave Him
behind without his Parents confent.

At

At laft, when My Lord took his leave of the Duke, the Duke being a very generous perfon, prefented Him with a *Spanifh* Horfe, a Saddle very richly embroidered, and with a rich Jewel of Diamonds.

Some time after My Lord's return into *England*, *Gilbert* Earl of *Shrewsbury* died, and left My Lord, though he was then but young, and about Twenty two years of age, his Executor; a year after, his Father Sir *Charles Cavendifh*, died alfo. His Mother, being then a Widow, was defirous that My Lord fhould marry : in obedience to whofe Commands, he chofe a Wife both to his own good liking, and his Mothers approving; who was Daughter and Heir to *William Baffet* of *Blore* Efq; a very honourable and ancient Family in *Stafford-fhire*, by whom was added a great part to His Eftate, as hereafter fhall be mentioned. After My Lord was married, he lived, for the moft part, in the Country, and pleafed Himfelf and his neighbours with Hofpitality, and fuch delights as the Country afforded; onely now and then he would go up to *London* for fome fhort time to wait on the King.

About this time King *James*, of bleffed memory, having a purpofe to confer fome Honour upon My Lord, made him Vifcount *Mansfield*, and Baron of *Bolfover*; and after the deceafe of King *James*, King *Charles* the Firft, of bleffed Memory, conftituted him Lord Warden of the Forreft of *Sherewood*, and Lieutenant

tenant of *Nottingham-shire*, and restored his Mother *Catharine*, the second Daughter of *Cuthbert* Lord *Ogle*, to her Fathers Dignity, after the death of her onely Sister *Jane* Countess of *Shrewsbury*, publickly declaring, that it was her Right ; which Title after the death of his Mother, descended also upon My Lord, and his Heirs General, together with a large Inheritance of 3000 l. a year, in *Northumberland.*

About the same time, after the decease of *William*, late Earl of *Devonshire*, his Noble Cousin German, My Lord was by his said Majesty made Lord Lieutenant of *Derby-shire* ; which trust and honour, after he had enjoyed for several years, and managed it, like as all other offices put to his Trust, with all possible care, faithfulness and dexterity, during the time of the said Earls Son, *William* the now Earl of *Devonshire*, his Minority, as soon as this same Earl was come to age, and by Law made capable of that trust, he willingly and freely resign'd it into his hands, he having hitherto kept it onely for him, that he and no body else might succeed his Father in that dignity.

In these, and all other both publick and private imployments, My Lord hath ever been careful to keep up the Kings Rights to the uttermost of his power, to strengthen those mentioned Counties with Ammunition, and to administer Justice to every one; for he refused no mans Petition, but sent all that came to him either for relief or justice, away from him fully satisfied.   C   Not

Not long after his being made Lieutenant of *Nottingham-shire*, there was found so great a defect of Armes and Ammunition in that County, that the Lords of the Council being advertised thereof, as the manner then was, His Majesty commanded a levy to be made upon the whole County for the supply thereof; whereupon the sum of 500 l. or thereabout, was accordingly levied for that purpose, and three Persons of Quality, then Deputy Lieutenants, were desired by My Lord to receive the money, and see it disposed; which being done accordingly, and a certain account rendred to My Lord, he voluntarily ordered the then Clerk of the Peace of that County, That the same account should be recorded amongst the Sessions Roles, and be published in open Sessions, to the end that the Country might take notice, how their monies were disposed of; for which act of Justice My Lord was highly commended.

Within some few years after, King *Charles* the First, of blessed Memory, His Gracious Soveraign, in regard of His true and faithful service to his King and Country, was pleased to honour him with the Title of *Earl of Newcastle*, and *Baron of Bothal* and *Heple*; which Title he graced so much by His Noble Actions and Deportments, that some seven years after, which was in the Year 1638. His Majesty called him up to Court, and thought Him the fittest Person whom He might intrust with the Government

of

of His Son *Charles* then Prince of *Wales*, now our
moſt Gracious King, and made him withal a Member
of the Lords of His Majeſties moſt honourable Privy
Council; which, as it was a great Honour and Truſt,
ſo He ſpared no care and induſtry to diſcharge His
Duty accordingly; and to that end, left all the care
of governing his own Family and Eſtate, with all Fidelity attending His Maſter not without conſiderable
Charges, and vaſt Expences of his own.

In this preſent Employment He continued for the
ſpace of three Years, during which time there happened an Inſurrection and Rebellion of His Majeſties
diſcontented Subjects in *Scotland*, which forced His
Majeſty to raiſe an Army, to reduce them to their O-
bedience, and His Treaſury being at that time ex-
hauſted, he was neceſſitated to deſire ſome ſupply and
aſſiſtance of the Nobleſt and Richeſt of his Loyal
Subjects; amongſt the reſt, My Lord lent His Majeſty 10000 l. and raiſed Himſelf a Voluntier-Troop
of Horſe, which conſiſted of 120 Knights and Gentlemen of Quality, who marched to *Berwick* by His
Majeſties Command, where it pleaſed His Majeſty to
ſet this mark of Honour upon that Troop, that it
ſhould be Independent, and not commanded by any
General Officer, but onely by his Majeſty Himſelf;
The reaſon thereof was upon this following occa-
ſion.

His Majesties whole body of Horse, being commanded to march into *Scotland* againſt the Rebels, a place was appointed for their Rendezvous; Immediately upon their meeting, My Lord ſent a Gentleman of Quality of his Troop * to His Majesties then General of the Horse, to know where his Troop ſhould march; who returned this anſwer, That it was to march next after the Troops of the General Officers of the Field. My Lord conceiving that his Troop ought to march in the Van, and not in the Rear, ſent the ſame Meſſenger back again to the General, to inform him, That he had the honour to march with the Princes Colours, and therefore he thought it not fit to march under any of the Officers of the Field ; yet neverthelefs the General ordered that Troop as he had formerly directed. Whereupon, My Lord thinking it unfit at that time to diſpute the bufineſs, immediately commanded his Cornet * to take off the Princes Colours from his ſtaff, and ſo marched in the place appointed, chooſing rather to march without his Colours flying, then to leſſen his Maſters dignity by the command of any ſubject.

*Sir *William* Carnaby, Kt.

* Mr. *Gray*, Brother to the Lord *Gray* of the North.

Immediately after the return from that expedition to his Majesties Leaguer, the General made a complaint thereof to his Majeſty ; who being truly informed of the bufineſs, commended my Lords diſcretion for it, and from that time ordered that Troop to be commanded by none but himſelf. Thus they remain'd

████████████████████, until His Majesty had reduced his Rebellious Subjects, and then My Lord returned with honour to his Charge, *viz*. The Government of the Prince.

At last when the whole Army was disbanded, then, and not before, my Lord thought it a fit Time to exact an account from the said General for the affront he pass'd upon him, and sent him a Challenge; the place and hour being appointed by both their Consents, where and when to meet, My Lord appear'd there with his Second *, but found not his Opposite: After some while his Opposite's Second came all alone, by whom my Lord perceiv'd that their Design had been discover'd to the King by some of his Opposite's Friends, who presently caused them both to be confined until he had made their Peace. * Francis Palmes.

My Lord having hitherto attended the Prince, his Master, with all faithfulness and duty befitting so great an Employment, for the space of three years, in the beginning of that Rebellious and unhappy Parliament, which was the cause of all the ruines and misfortunes that afterwards befell this Kingdom, was privately advertised, that the Parliaments Design was to take the Government of the Prince from him, which he apprehending as a disgrace to Himself, wisely prevented, and obtained the Consent of His late Majesty, with His Favour, to deliver up the

D   Charge

Charge of being Governor to the Prince, and retire into the Countrey; which he did in the beginning of the Year 1641, and setled himself, with his Lady, Children and Family, to his great satisfaction, with an intent to have continued there, and rested under his own Vine, and managed his own Estate; but he had not enjoyed himself long, but an Express came to him from His Majesty, who was then unjustly and unmannerly treated by the said Parliament, to repair with all possible speed and privacy, to *Kingston* upon *Hull*, where the greatest part of His Majesties Ammunition and Arms then remained in that Magazine, it being the most considerable place for strength in the Northern parts of the Kingdom.

Immediately upon the receipt of these His Majesties Orders and Commands, my Lord prepared for their execution, and about Twelve of the Clock at night, hastned from his own house when his Familie were all at their rest, save two or three Servants which he appointed to attend him. The next day early in the morning he arrived at *Hull*, in the quality of a private Gentleman, which place was distant from his house forty miles; and none of his Family that were at home, knew what was become of him, till he sent an Express to his Lady to inform her where he was.

Thus

Thus being admitted into the Town, he fell upon his intended Design, and brought it to so hopeful an issue for His Majesties Service, that he wanted nothing but His Majesties further Commission and Pleasure to have secured both the Town and Magazine for His Majesties use; and to that end by a speedy Express * gave His Majesty, who was then at *Windsor*, an account of all his Transactions therein, together with his Opinion of them, hoping His Majesty would have been pleased either to come thither in Person, which He might have done with much security, or at least have sent him a Commission and Orders how he should do His Majesty further Service.

* Capt. Mazine.

But instead thereof he received Orders from His Majesty to observe such Directions as he should receive from the Parliament then sitting: Whereupon he was summoned personally to appear at the House of Lords, and a Committee chosen to examine the Grounds and Reasons of his undertaking that Design; but my Lord shewed them his Commission, and that it was done in obedience to His Majesties Commands, and so was cleared of that Action.

Not long after, my Lord obtained the freedom from His Majesty to retire again to his Countrey-Life, which he did with much alacrity: He had not remained many months there, but His Majesty

was

was forced by the fury of the said Parliament, to repair in Person to *York*, and to send the Queen beyond the Seas for her safety.

No sooner was His Majesty arrived at *York*, but he sent his Commands to my Lord to come thither to him; which according to his wonted custom and loyalty he readily obeyed, and after a few days spent there in Consultation, His Majesty was pleased to Command him to *Newcastle* upon *Tyne*, to take upon him the Government of that Town, and the four Counties next adjoining; that is to say, *Northumberland*, *Cumberland*, *Westmerland*, and the Bishoprick of *Durham*: which my Lord did accordingly, although he wanted Men, Money and Ammunition, for the performance of that design; for when he came thither, he neither found any Military provision considerable for the undertaking that work, nor generally any great encouragement from the people in those parts, more then what his own interest created in them; Neverthelefs, he thought it his duty rather to hazard all, then to neglect the Commands of His Soveraign; and resolved to shew his Fidelity, by nobly setting all at stake, as he did, though he well knew how to have secured himself, as too many others did, either by Neutrality, or adhering to the Rebellious Party; but his Honour and Loyalty was too great to be stained with such foul adherencies.

As

As soon as my Lord came to *Newcastle*, in the first place he sent for all his Tenants and Friends in those parts, and presently raised a Troop of Horse consisting of 120. and a Regiment of Foot, and put them under Command, and upon duty and exercise in the Town of *Newcastle* ; and with this small beginning took the Government of that place upon him ; where with the assistance of the Towns-men, particularly the Mayor,* (whom by the power of his Forces, he continued Mayor for the year following, he being a person of much trust and fidelity, as he approved himself) and the rest of his Brethren, within few days he fortified the Town, and raised men daily, and put a Garrison of Soldiers into *Tinmouth*-Castle, standing upon the River *Tyne*, betwixt *Newcastle* and the Sea, to secure that Port, and armed the Soldiers as well as he could : And thus he stood upon his Guard, and continued them upon Duty ; playing his weak Game with much Prudence, and giving the Town and Country very great satisfaction by his noble and honourable Deportment.

* *Sir John Marlay* Kt.

In the mean time, there happend a great mutiny of the Trainband Souldiers of the Bishoprick at *Durham*, so that my Lord was forced to remove thither in Person, attended with some forces to appease them ; where at his arrival (I mention it by the way, and as a merry passage) a jovial Fellow used this expression, That he liked my Lord very well ; but

E   not

not his Company (meaning his Soldiers.)

After my Lord had reduced them to their obedience and duty, he took great care of the Church Government in the said Bishoprick (as he did no less in
all other places committed to his Care and Protection,
well knowing that Schism and Faction in Religion is
the Mother of all or most Rebellions, Wars and Disturbances in a State or Government) and constituted
that Learned and Eminent Divine the then Dean of
* Dr. Coo- *Peterborough,* now Lord-Bishop of *Durham* *, to view
sens. all Sermons that were to be Preached, and suffer nothing in them that in the least reflected against His Majesties Person and Government, but to put forth and
add whatsoever he thought convenient, and punish
those that should trespass against it. In which that
worthy Person used so much care and industry, that
never the Church could be more happily govern'd
then it was at that present.

Some short time after, my Lord received from Her
Majesty the Queen, out of *Holland* a small supply of
Money, *viz.* a little barrel of Ducatoons, which
amounted to about 500 l. *Sterling*; which my Lord
distributed amongst the Officers of his new raised Army, to encourage them the better in their service; as
also some Armes, the most part whereof were consign-
ed to his late Majesty; and those that were ordered to
be conveyed to his Majesty, were sent accordingly,
conducted by that onely Troop of Horse, which my
Lord

Lord had newly raifed, with orders to return again
to him; but it feems His Majefty liked the Troop fo
well, that he was pleafed to command their ftay to recruit his own Army.

About the fame time the King of *Denmark* was likewife pleafed to fend His Majefty a Ship, which arrived at *Newcaftle*, laden with fome Ammunition,
Armes, Regiment Pieces, and *Danifh* Clubs; which
my Lord kept for the furnifhing of fome Forces which
he intended to raife for His Majefties fervice; for he
perceiving the flames increafe more and more in both
the Houfes of Parliament then fitting at *Weftminfter*,
againft his Majefties Perfon and Government; upon
Confultation with his Friends and Allies, and the intereft he had in thofe Northern parts, took a refolution to raife an Army for His Majefties fervice, and
by an exprefs acquainted His Majefty with his defign;
who was fo well pleafed with it, that he fent him Com-
miffions for that purpofe, to conftitute him General
of all the Forces raifed and to be raifed in all the parts
of the Kingdom, *Trent-North*, and moreover in the
feveral Counties of *Lincoln, Nottingham, Derby, Lan-
cafhire, Chefhire, Leicefter, Rutland, Cambridg, Huntington, Norfolk, Suffolk*, and *Effex*, and Commander
in Chief for the fame; as alfo to impower and autho-
rize him to confer the honour of Knighthood upon
fuch Perfons as he fhould conceive deferved it, and
to coin Money and Print whenfoever he faw occafion
for

for it : Which as it was not onely a great Honour,
but a great Truſt and Power ; ſo he uſed it with much
diſcretion and wiſdom, onely in ſuch occurrencies,
where he found it tending to the advancement of His
Majeſties Service, and conferr'd the honour of Knighthood ſparingly, and but on ſuch perſons, whoſe Valiant and Loyal Actions did juſtly deſerve it, ſo that
he Knighted in all to the number of Twelve.

Within a ſhort time, my Lord formed an Army
of 8000 Foot, Horſe and Dragoons, and put them
into a condition to march in the beginning of *November* 1642. No ſooner was this effected, but the Inſurrection grew high in *York-ſhire*, in ſo much, that
moſt of His Majeſties good ſubjects of that County,
as well the Nobility as Gentry, were forced for the
preſervation of their perſons, to retire to the City of
York, a walled Town, but of no great ſtrength; and
hearing that my Lord had not onely kept thoſe Counties in the Northen parts generally faithful to his Majeſty, but raiſed an Army for His Majeſties Intereſt,
and the protection of his good ſubjects ; thought it
convenient to employ and authoriſe ſome perſons of
Quality to attend upon my Lord, and treat with
him on their behalf, that he would be pleaſed to give
them the aſſiſtance of his Army, which my Lord granted them upon ſuch Terms as did highly advance His
Majeſties Service, which was my Lords chief and onely aim.

Thus

Thus my Lord being with his Army invited into *York-ſhire*, He prepared for it with all the ſpeed that the nature of that buſineſs could poſſibly permit; and after he had fortified the Town of *Newcaſtle*, *Tynmouthcaſtle*, *Hartlepool* (a Haven Town) and ſome other neceſſary Gariſons in thoſe parts, and Mann'd, Victuall'd and order'd their conſtant ſupply, He thought it fit in the firſt place, before he did march, to manifeſt to the World by a Declaration in Print, the reaſons and grounds of his undertaking that deſign; which were in General, for the preſervation of His Majeſties Perſon and Government, and the defence of the Orthodox Church of *England*; where He alſo ſatisfied thoſe that murmur'd for my Lords receiving into his Army ſuch as were of the Catholick Religion, and then he preſently marched with his Army into *York-ſhire* to their aſſiſtance, and within the time agreed upon, came to *York*, notwithſtanding the Enemies Forces gave him all the interruption they poſſibly could, at ſeveral paſſes; whereof the chief was at *Pierce-bridg*, at the entering into *York-ſhire*, where 1500 of the Enemies Forces, Commanded in chief by Col. *Hotham*, were ready to interrupt my Lord's Forces, ſent thither to ſecure that paſſe, conſiſting of a Regiment of Dragoons, commanded by Colonel *Thomas Howard*, and a Regiment of Foot, Commanded by Sir *William Lambton*, which they performed with ſo much Courage, that they routed the

F   Enemy

Enemy, and put them to flight, although the said
Col. *Howard* in that Charge loft his life by an unfortunate fhot.

The Enemy thus miffing of their defign, fled until they met with a conjunction of their whole Forces at *Tadcafter*, fome eight miles diftant from *York*,
and my Lord went on without any other confiderable Interruption. Being come to *York*, he drew up
his whole Army before the Town, both Horfe and
Foot, where the Commander in Chief, the then
Earl of *Cumberland*, together with the Gentry of
the Country, came to wait on my Lord, and the
then Governor of *York*, Sir *Thomas Glemham*, prefented him with the Keys of the City.

Thus my Lord marched into the Town with great
joy, and to the general fatisfaction both of the
Nobility and Gentry, and moft of the Citizens;
and immediately without any delay, in the later end
of *December* 1642, fell upon Confultations how
he might beft proceed to ferve his King and Country; and particularly, how his Army fhould be
maintained and paid, (as he did alfo afterwards in
every Country wherefoever he marched) well knowing, that no Army can be governed without being
conftantly and regularly fupported by provifion and
pay. Whereupon it was agreed, That the Nobility and Gentry of the feveral Counties, fhould fe-
lect a certain number of themfelves to raife money
by

by a regular Tax, for the making provifions for the
fupport and maintenance of the Army, rather than
to leave them to free-quarter, and to carve for themfelves; and if any of the Soldiers were exorbitant
and diforderly, and that it did appear fo to thofe
that were authorifed to examine their deportment,
that prefently order fhould be given to repair thofe
injuries out of the moneys levied for the Soldiery;
by which means the Country was preferved from
many inconveniences, which otherwife would doubtlefs have followed.

And though the feafon of the year might well have
invited my Lord to take up his Winter-quarters, it
being about *Chriftmas*; yet after he had put a good
Garifon into the City of *York*, and fortified it, upon intelligence that the Enemy was ftill at *Tadcafter*,
and had fortified that place, he refolved to march
thither. The greateft part of the Town ftands on the
Weft fide of a River not fordable in any place near
thereabout, nor allowing any paffage into the Town
from *York*, but over a Stone-bridge, which the E-
nemy had made impaffable by breaking down part
of the Bridg, and planting their Ordnance upon it,
and by raifing a very large and ftrong Fort upon the
top of a Hill, leading Eaftward from that Bridg
towards *York*, upon defign of commanding the Bridg
and all other places fit to draw up an Army in, or to
plant Cannon againft them.

But

But notwithstanding all these Discouragements, my Lord after he had refresh'd his Army at *York*, and recruited his provisions, ordered a march before the said Town in this manner: That the greatest part of his Horse and Dragoons should in the night march to a Pass at *Weatherby*, five miles distant from *Tadcaster*, towards North-west, from thence under the Command of his then Lieutenant General of the Army, to appear on the West side of *Tadcaster* early the next morning, by which time my Lord with the rest of his Army resolved to appear at the East-side of the said Town; which intention was well design'd, but ill executed; for though my Lord with that part of the Army which he commanded in person, that is to say, his Foot and Cannon, attended by some Troops of Horse, did march that night, and early in the morning appear'd before the Town on the East side thereof, and there drew up his Army, planted his Cannon, and closely and orderly besieged that side of the Town, and from ten in the morning till four a Clock in the afternoon, battered the Enemies Forts and Works, as being in continual expectation of the appearance of the Troops on the other side, according to his order; yet (whether it was out of Neglect or Treachery that my Lords Orders were not obeyed) that days Work was rendred ineffectual as to the whole Design.

However the vigilancy of My Lord did put the Enemy into such a Terror, that they forsook that Fort, and secretly fled away with all their Train that very night to another strong hold not far distant from *Tadcaster*, called *Cawood*-Castle, to which, by reason of its low and boggy Scituation, and foul and narrow Lanes and passages, it was not possible for my Lord to pursue them without too great an hazard to his Army; whereas had the Lieutenant General performed his Duty, in all probability the greatest part of the principal Rebels in *York-shire*, would that day have been taken in their own trap, and their further mischief prevented. My Lord, the next morning, instead of storming the Town, (as he had intended) entred without interruption, and there stayed some few days to refresh his Army, and order that part of the Country.

In *December* 1642. My Lord thought it fit to march to *Pomfret*, and to quarter his Army in that part of the Country, which was betwixt *Cawood*, and some Garisons of the Enemy, in the west part of *York-shire*, *viz. Hallifax*, *Bradford*, *Leeds*, *Wakefield*, &c. where he remained some time to recruit and enlarge his Army, which was much lessened by erecting of Garisons, and to keep those parts in order and obedience to His Majesty; And after he had thus ordered his Affairs, He was enabled to give Protection to those parts of the Country that were most willing to embrace it, and

G   quarter'd

quarter'd his Army for a time in such places which he had reduced. *Tadcaster*, which stood upon a Pass, he made a Garison, or rather a strong Quarter, and put also a Garison into *Pomfret* Castle, not above eight Miles distant from *Tadcaster*, which commanded that Town, and a great part of the Country.

During the time that his Army remained at *Pomfret*, My Lord setled a Garison at *Newark* in *Nottingham-shire*, standing upon the River *Trent*, a very considerable pass, which kept the greatest part of *Nottingham-shire*, and part of *Lincoln-shire* in obedience; and after that, he returned in the beginning of *January* 1642, back to *York*, with an intention to supply Himself with some Ammunition, which He had ordered to be brought from *Newcastle*: A Convoy of Horse that were imployed to conduct it from thence, under the Command of the Lieutenant General of the Army the Lord *Ethyn*, was by the Enemy at a pass, called *Tarum-bridg*, in *York-shire*, fiercely encountred; in which encounter My Lord's Forces totally routed them, slew many, and took many Prisoners, and most of their Horse Colours consisting of Seventeen Cornets; and so march'd on to *York* with their Ammunition, without any other Interruption.

My Lord, after he had received this Ammunition, put his Army into a condition to march, and having intelligence that the Queen was at Sea, with intention to land in some part of the Eastriding of *York-shire*, he
directed

directed his March in *February* 1642, into those parts, to be ready to attend Her Majesties landing, who was then daily expected from *Holland*. Within a short time, after it had pleased God to protect Her Majesty both from the fury of Wind and Waves, there being for several days such a Tempest at Sea, that Her Majesty, with all her Attendance, was in danger to be cast away every minute; as also from the fury of the Rebels, which had the whole Naval Power of the Kingdom then in their Hands: she arrived safely at a small Port in the Eastriding of *York-shire*, called *Burlington* Key, where Her Majesty was no sooner landed, but the Enemy at Sea made continual shot against her Ships in the Port, which reached not onely Her Majesties landing, but even the House where she lay (though without the least hurt to any) so that she her self, and her Attendants, were forced to leave the same, and to seek Protection from a Hill near that place, under which they retired; and all that while it was observed, that Her Majesty shewed as much Courage as ever any person could do; for Her undaunted and Generous spirit was like her Royal Birth, deriving it self from that unparrallell'd King, Her Father, whose Heroick Actions will be in perpetual Memory, whilest the World hath a being.

My Lord finding Her Majesty in this condition, drew his Army near the place where she was, ready to attend and protect Her Majesties Person, who

was

was pleased to take a view of the Army as it was drawn up in order; and immediately after, which was in *March* 1643, took Her journey towards *York*, whither the whole Army conducted Her Majesty, and brought her safe into the City. About this time, Her Majesty having some present occasion for Money, My Lord presented Her with 3000 l. *Sterling*, which she graciously accepted of, and having spent some time there in Consultation about the present affairs, she was pleased to send some Armes and Ammunition to the King, who was then in *Oxford*; to which end, my Lord ordered a Party consisting of 1500, well Commanded, to conduct the same, with whom the Lord *Percy*, who then had waited upon Her Majesty from the King, returned to *Oxford*; which Party His Majesty was pleased to keep with him for his own Service.

Not long after, My Lord, who always endeavoured to win any place or persons by fair means, rather then by using of force, reduced to His Majesties obedience a strong Fort and Castle upon the Sea, and a very good Haven, call'd *Scarborough*-Castle, perswading the Governour thereof, who heretofore had opposed his Forces at *Yarum*-bridg, with such rational and convincible Arguments, that he willingly rendred himself, and all the Garison, unto His Majesties Devotion; By which prudent Action My Lord highly advanced His Majesties Interest; for by that means the Enemy was much annoyed and prejudiced

at

at Sea, and a great part in the Eaſt-riding of *York-ſhire*
kept in due obedience.

After this, My Lord having received Intelligence
that the Enemies General of the Horſe* had deſigned
to march with a Party from *Cawood* Caſtle, whither
they were fled from *Tadcaſter*, as before is mentioned,
to ſome Gariſons which they had in the Weſt of
York-ſhire; preſently order'd a party of Horſe, Commanded by the General of the Horſe, the Lord *George
Goring*, to attend the Enemy in their March, who o-
vertook them on a Moor, call'd *Seacroft-Moor*, and
fell upon their Rear, which cauſed the Enemy to draw
up their Forces into a Body; to whom they gave a
Total rout (although their number was much greater)
and took about 800 Priſoners, and 10 or 12 Colours
of Horſe, beſides many that were ſlain in the charge;
which Priſoners were brought to *York*, about 10 or 12
miles diſtant from that ſame place.

Immediately after, in purſuit of that Victory, My
Lord ſent a conſiderable Party into the Weſt of *York-
ſhire*, where they met with about 2000 of the Enemies Forces, taken out of their ſeveral Gariſons in
thoſe parts, to execute ſome deſign upon a Moor called *Tankerly-Moor*, and there fought them, and routed
them; many were ſlain, and ſome taken Priſoners.

Not long after, the Remainder of the Army that
were left at *York*, marched to *Leeds*, in the Weſt of
York-ſhire, and from thence to *Wakefield*, being both

H   the

*Sir Tho-
mas Fair-
fax.*

the Enemies Quarters, to reduce and fettle that part of the Country : My Lord having poffeffed himfelf of the Town of *Wakefield*, it being large, and of great compafs, and able to make a ftrong quarter, order'd it accordingly; and receiving Intelligence that in two Market-Towns Southweft from *Wakefield*, *viz*. *Rotheram* and *Sheffield*, the Enemy was very bufie to raife Forces againft his Majefty, and had fortified them both about four miles diftant from each other, hoping thereby to give protection and encouragement to all thofe parts of the Country which were populous, rich and rebellious, he thought it neceffary to ufe his beft endeavours to blaft thofe their wicked defigns in the bud; and thereupon took a refolution in *April* 1643, to march with part of his Army from *Wakefield* into the mentioned parts, attended with a convenient Train of Artillery and Ammunition, leaving the greateft part of it at *Wakefield* with the remainder of his Army, under the Care and Conduct of his General of the Horfe, and Major General of the Army *, which was fo confiderable, both in refpect of their number and provifion, that they did, as they might well, conceive themfelves Mafter of the Field in thofe parts, and fecure in that quarter, although in the end it proved not fo, as fhall hereafter be declared, which muft neceffarily be imputed to their invigilancy and carelefsnefs.

My

My Lord first marched to *Rotheram*, and finding that the Enemy had placed a Garison of Soldiers in that Town, and fortified it, he drew up his Army in the morning against the Town, and summon'd it; but they refusing to yield, my Lord fell to work with his Cannon and Musket, and within a short time took it by storm, and enter'd the Town that very night; some Enemies of note that were found therein, were taken Prisoners; and as for the common Soldiers, which were by the Enemy forced from their Allegiance, he shew'd such Clemency to them, that very many willingly took up Arms for His Majesties Service, and proved very faithful and loyal Subjects, and good Soldiers.

After my Lord had stayed two or three dayes there, and order'd those parts, he marched with his Army to *Sheffield*, another Market-Town of large extent, in which there was an ancient Castle; which when the Enemies Forces that kept the Town, came to hear of, being terrified with the fame of my Lords hitherto Victorious Army, they fled away from thence into *Derbyshire*, and left both Town and Castle (without any blow) to my Lords Mercy; and though the people in the Town were most of them rebelliously affected, yet my Lord so prudently ordered the business, that within a short time he reduced most of them to their Allegiance by love,

and

and the reſt by fear, and recruited his Army daily; he put a Gariſon of Soldiers into the Caſtle,
and fortified it in all reſpects, and conſtituted a Gen-
Sir *W. il.* tleman of Quality * Governour both of the Caſtle,
Savil Kt. Town and Country; and finding near that place
and Bar. ſome Iron Works, he gave preſent order for the
caſting of Iron Cannon for his Gariſons, and for
the making of other Inſtruments and Engines of
War.

Within a ſhort time after, my Lord receiving
Intelligence that the Enemy in the Gariſons near
Wakefield had united themſelves, and being drawn
into a body in the night time, had ſurpriſed and enter'd the Town of *Wakefield*, and taken all or moſt
of the Officers and Soldiers, left there, Priſoners,
(amongſt whom was alſo the General of the Horſe,
the Lord *Goring*, whom my Lord afterwards redeem'd
by Exchange) and poſſeſſed themſelves of the whole
Magazine, which was a very great loſs and hinderance
to my Lords deſigns, it being the Moity of his
Army, and moſt of his Ammunition, he fell upon new Counſels, and reſolved without any delay
to march from thence back towards *York*, which was
in *May* 1643, where after he had reſted ſome time,
Her Majeſty being reſolved to take Her Journey towards the Southern parts of the Kingdom, where the
King was, deſigned firſt to go from *York* to *Pomfret*,
whither my Lord ordered the whole Marching *Army*

to

to be in readiness to conduct Her Majesty, which they did, he himself attending Her Majesty in person. And after Her Majesty had rested there some small time, she being desirous to proceed in Her intended Journey, no less then a formed Army was able to secure Her Person: Wherefore my Lord was resolved out of his fidelity and duty to supply Her with an Army of 7000 Horse and Foot, besides a convenient Train of Artillery, for Her safer Conduct; chusing rather to leave himself in a weak condition (though he was even then very near the Enemies Garisons in that part of the Country) then suffer Her Majesties Person to be exposed to danger. Which Army of 7000 men, when Her Majesty was safely arrived to the King, He was pleased to keep with him for His own Service.

After Her Majesties departure out of *Yorkshire*, my Lord was forced to recruit again his Army, and within a short time, *viz.* in *June* 1643, took a resolution to march into the Enemies Quarters, in the Western parts; in which march he met with a strong stone house well fortified, call'd *Howley*-House, wherein was a Garison of Soldiers, which my Lord summon'd; but the Governour disobeying the summons, he batter'd it with his Cannon, and so took it by force; the Governour having quarter given him contrary to my Lords Orders, was brought before my Lord by a Person of Quality, for which the Offi-

I   cer

cer that brought him, received a check; and though
he resolved then to kill him, yet my Lord would
not suffer him to do it, saying, It was inhumane
to kill any man in cold blood. Hereupon the Governour kiss'd the Key of the House door, and presented it to my Lord; to which my Lord return'd
this answer, *I need it not*, said he, *for I brought a*
Key along with me, which yet I was unwilling to use,
until you forced me to it.

At this House my Lord remained five or six days,
till he had refreshed his Soldiers; and then a resolution was taken to march against a Garison of the
Enemies call'd *Bradford*, a little, but a strong Town;
in the way he met with a strong interruption by the
Enemy drawing forth a vast number of Musquetiers, which they had very privately gotten out of
Lancashire, the next adjoining County to those parts
of *York-shire*, which had so easie an access to them at
Bradford, by reason the whole Country was of their
Party, that my Lord could not possibly have any
constant intelligence of their designs and motions; for
in their Army there were near 5000 Musquetiers, and
18 Troops of Horse, drawn up in a place full of hedges,
called *Atherton-moor*, near to their Garison at *Brad-*
ford, ready to encounter my Lords Forces, which
then contained not above half so many Musquetiers
as the Enemy had; their chiefest strength consisting
in Horse, and these made useless for a long time together

gether, by the Enemies Horse possessing all the plain
ground upon that Field ; so that no place was left to
draw up my Lords Horse, but amongst old Coal-
pits : Neither could they charge the Enemy, by reason of a great ditch and high bank betwixt my Lord's
and the Enemies Troops, but by two on a breast,
and that within Musquet shot ; the Enemy being
drawn up in hedges, and continually playing upon
them, which rendred the service exceeding difficult and
hazardous.

In the mean while the Foot of both sides on the
right and left Wings, encounter'd each other, who
fought from Hedg to Hedg, and for a long time
together overpower'd and got ground of my Lords
Foot, almost to the invironing of his Cannon; my
Lords Horse (wherein consisted his greatest strength)
all this while being made, by reason of the ground,
incapable of charging ; at last the Pikes of my Lords
Army having had no employment all the day, were
drawn against the Enemies left wing, and particularly those of my Lords own Regiment, which
were all stout and valiant men, who fell so furiously
upon the Enemy, that they forsook their hedges, and
fell to their heels: At which very instant, my Lord caused a shot or two to be made by his Cannon against the
Body of the Enemies Horse, drawn up within Cannon
shot, which took so good effect, that it disordered the
Enemies Troops ; Hereupon my Lord's Horse got

over

over the Hedg, not in a body (for that they could
not) but difperfedly two on a breaft; and as foon as
fome confiderable number was gotten over, and drawn
up, they charged the Enemy, and routed them; fo
that in an inftant there was a ftrange change of Fortune, and the Field totally won by my Lord, notwithftanding he had quitted 7000 Men, to conduct Her
Majefty, befides a good Train of Artillery, which in
fuch a Conjuncture would have weakned *Cæfars* Army. In this Victory the Enemy loft moft of their
Foot, about 3000 were taken Prifoners, and 700
Horfe and Foot flain, and thofe that efcaped, fled into their Garifon at *Bradford,* amongft whom was alfo
their General of the Horfe.

After this, My Lord caufed his Army to be rallied,
and marched in order that night before *Bradford,* with
an intention to ftorm it the next morning ; but the
Enemy that were in the Town, it feems, were fo dif-
comfited, that the fame night they efcaped all various
ways, and amongft them the faid General of the Horfe,
whofe Lady being behind a Servant on Horfe-back,
was taken by fome of My Lord's Soldiers and brought
to his Quarters, where fhe was treated and attended with all civility and refpect, and within few days
fent to *York* in my Lords own Coach, and from
thence very fhortly after to *Kingftone* upon *Hull,*
where fhe defired to be, attended by my Lords
Coach and Servants.

Thus

Thus my Lord, after the Enemy was gone, entred the Town and Garifon of *Bradford*, by which
Victory the Enemy was fo daunted, that they for-
fook the reft of their Garifons, that is to fay, *Hallifax*, *Leeds* and *Wakefield*, and difperfed themfelves
feverally, the chief Officers retiring to *Hull*, a ftrong
Garifon of the Enemy; and though my Lord, knowing they would make their efcape thither, as having
no other place of refuge to refort to, fent a Letter
to *York* to the Governour of that City, to ftop them
in their paffage; yet by neglect of the Poft, it coming not timely enough to his hands, his Defign was
fruftrated.

The whole County of *York*, fave onely *Hull*,
being now cleared and fetled by my Lords Care and
Conduct, he marched to the City of *York*, and having a competent number of Horfe well armed and
commanded, he quarter'd them in the Eaft-riding,
near *Hull*, there being no vifible Enemy then to oppofe them: In the mean while my Lord receiving
News that the Enemy had made an Invafion into the
next adjoining County of *Lincoln*, where he had
fome Forces, he prefently difpatched * his Lieutenant General of the Army away with fome Horfe
and Dragoons, and foon after marched thither himfelf with the body of the Army, being earneftly
defired by his Majefties Party there. The Forces
which my Lord had in the fame County, command-

* The Lord *Ethyn*.

K   ed

ed by the then Lieutenant General of the Horse, Mr.
Charles Cavendish, second Brother to the now Earl
of *Devonshire*, though they had timely notice, and
Orders from my Lord to make their retreat to the
Lieutenant-General of the Army, and not to fight
the Enemy ; yet the said Lieutenant-General of the
Horse being transported by his Courage, (he being
a Person of great Valour and Conduct) and having
charged the Enemy, unfortunately lost the field, and
himself was slain in the Charge, his Horse lighting in a
bogg : Which news being brought to my Lord when
he was on his March, he made all the haste he could,
and was no sooner joined with his Lieutenant General, but fell upon the Enemy, and put them to
flight.

The first Garison my Lord took in *Lincolnshire*,
was *Gainsborrough*, a Town standing upon the River *Trent*, wherein (not long before) had been a
Garison of Soldiers for His Majesty, under the Command of the then Earl of *Kingstone*, but surprised,
and the Town Taken by the Enemies Forces, who
having an intention to conveigh the said Earl of
Kingstone from thence to *Hull* in a little Pinnace,
met with some of my Lords Forces by the way,
commanded by the Lieutenant of the Army, who
being desirous to rescue the Earl of *Kingstone*, and
making some shots with their Regiment Pieces,
to stop the Pinnace, unfortunately slew him, and
one of his Servants.   My

My Lord drawing near the mentioned Town of
Gainsborrough, there appear'd on the top of a Hill
above the Town, some of the Enemies Horse drawn
up in a body; whereupon he immediately sent a
party of his Horse to view them; who no sooner
came within their sight, but they retreated fairly so
long as they could well endure; but the pursuit of
my Lords Horse caused them presently to break their
ranks, and fall to their heels; where most of them
escaped, and fled to *Lincoln*, another of their Gar-
risons. Hereupon my Lord summon'd the Town of
Gainsborrough; but the Governour thereof refusing
to yield, caused my Lord to plant his Cannon, and
draw up his Army on the mention'd Hill; and having play'd some little while upon the Town, put
the Enemy into such a terror, that the Governour
sent out, and offer'd the surrender of the Town upon fair terms, which my Lord thought fit rather to
embrace, then take it by force; and though according to the Articles of Agreement made between
them, both the Enemies Arms and the Keys of the
Town should have been fairly delivered to my Lord;
yet it being not performed as it was expected, the
Arms being in a confused manner thrown down, and
the Gates set wide open, the Prisoners that had been
kept in the Town, began first to plunder; which
my Lords Forces seeing, did the same, although it
was against my *Lords* will and orders.

After

After my Lord had thus reduced the Town, and
put a good Garifon of Soldiers into it, and better fortified it, he marched before *Lincoln*, and there he
entred with his Army without great difficulty, and
plac'd alfo a Garifon in it, and raifed a confiderable Army, both Horfe, Foot and Dragoons, for
the prefervation of that County, and put them under Commanders, and conftituted a Perfon of Honour * Commander in Chief, with intention to
march towards the South, which if it had taken effect, would doubtlefs have made an end of that War;
but he being daily importuned by the Nobility and
Gentry of *York-fhire*, to return into that County,
efpecially upon the perfwafions of the Commander
in Chief of the Forces left there, who acquainted
my Lord that the Enemy grew fo ftrong every day,
being got together in *Kingftone* upon *Hull*, and an-
noying that Country, that his Forces were not able
to bear up againft them; alledging withall, that my
Lord would be fufpected to betray the Truft repo-
fed in him, if he came not to fuccour and affift
them; he went back with his Army for the protection of that fame Country; and when he arrived
there, which was in *Auguft* 1643, he found the E-
nemy of fo fmall confequence, that they did all flie
before him. About this time His Majefty was pleafed to honour my Lord for His true and faithful
Service, with the Title of *Marquefs of Newcaftle*.

The Lord
*Widdring-
ton.*

My

My Lord being returned into *York-shire*, forced the Enemy first from a Town called *Beverly*, wherein they had a Garison of Soldiers; and from thence, upon the entreaty of the Nobility and Gentry of *York-shire*, (as before is mentioned) who promised him Ten thousand men for that purpose, though they came short of their performance, marched near the Town of *Kingstone* upon *Hull*, and besieged that part of the Garison that bordered on *York-shire*, for a certain time; in which time the Enemy took the courage to sally out of the Town with a strong party of Horse and Foot very early in the morning, with purpose to have forced the Quarters of a Regiment of my Lords Horse, that were quarter'd next the Town; but by the vigilancy of their Commander Sir *Marmaduke Langdale*, afterwards Lord *Langdale*, his Forces being prepared for their reception, they received such a Welcome as cost many of them their Lives, most of their Foot (but such as were slain) being taken Prisoners; and those of their Horse that escaped, got into their Hold at *Hull*.

The Enemy thus seeing that they could do my Lords Army no further damage on that side of the River in *York-shire*, endeavoured by all means(from *Hull*, and other confederate places in the Eastern parts of the Kingdom) to form a considerable party to annoy and disturb the Forces raised by my Lord in *Lincolnshire*, and left there for the protecti-

L

on

on of that County; where the Enemy being drawn
together in a body, fought my Lords Forces in his
abfence, and got the honour of the day near *Horn-
by* Caftle in that County; which lofs, caufed partly by their own rafhnefs, forced my Lord to leave
his defign upon *Hull*, and to march back with his
Army to *York*, which was in *October* 1643, where
he remained but a few dayes to refrefh his Army,
and receiving intelligence that the Enemy was got into *Derbyfhire*, and did grow numerous there, and
bufie in feducing the people, that Country being under my Lords Command, he refolved to direct his
March thither in the beginning of *November* 1643,
to fupprefs their further growth; and to that end
quarter'd his Army at *Chefterfield*, and in all the parts
thereabout, for a certain time.

Immediately after his departure from *York* to *Pomfret*, in his faid March into *Derbyfhire*, the City of
York fent to my Lord to inform him of their intention to chufe another Mayor for the year following,
defiring his pleafure about it : My Lord, who knew
that the Mayor for the year before, was a perfon
of much Loyalty and Difcretion, declared his mind
to them, That he thought it fit to continue him
Mayor alfo for the year following; which it feems
they did not like, but refolved to chufe one which
they pleafed, contrary to my Lords defire. My Lord
perceiving their intentions, about the time of the E-
lection,

lection sent orders to the Governour of the City of *York*, to permit such Forces to enter into the City as he should send; which being done accordingly, they upon the Day of the Election repaired to the Town-Hall, and with their Arms staid there until they had continued the said Mayor according to my Lords desire.

During the time of my Lords stay at *Chesterfield* in *Derbyshire*, he ordered some part of his Army to march before a strong House and Garison of the Enemies, call'd *Wingfield Mannor*, which in a short time they took by storm. And when my Lord had raised in that County as many Forces, Horse and Foot, as were supposed to be sufficient to preserve it from the fury of the Enemy, he armed them, and constituted an Honourable Person * Commander in Chief of all the Forces of that County, and of *Lei-cestershire*; and so leaving it in that condition, marched in *December* 1643, from *Chesterfield* to *Bolsover* in the same County, and from thence to *Welbeck* in *Nottinghamshire*, to his own House and Garison, in which parts he staid some time, both to refresh his Army, and to settle and reform some disorders he found there, leaving no visible Enemy behind him in *Derbyshire*, save onely an inconsiderable party in the Town of *Derby*, which they had fortified, not worth the labour to reduce it.

The Lord of *Lough-borrough*.

About

About this time the report came, that a great Army out of *Scotland*, was upon their march towards the Northern parts of *England*, to affift the Enemy against His Majefty, which forced the Nobility and Gentry of *Yorkfhire* to invite my Lord back again into thofe parts, with promife to raife for his fervice, an Army of 10000 men; My Lord (not upon this proffer, which had already heretofore deceived him, but out of his Loyalty and duty to preferve thofe parts which were committed to his care and protection) returned in the middle of *January* 1643. And when he came there, he found not one man raifed to affift him againft fo powerful an Army, nor an intention of raifing any; Wherefore he was neceffitated to raife himfelf, out of the Countrey, what forces he could get, and when he had fettled the affairs in *York-fhire* as well as time and his prefent condition would permit, and

The Lord
Bellafis. conftituted an honourable Perfon * Governor of *York* and Commander in chief of a very confiderable party of horfe and foot for the defence of the County (for Sr. *Thomas Glemham* was then made Colonel General, and marched into the Field with the Army) he took his march to *Newcaftle* in the beginning of *February* 1643, to give a ftop to the *Scots* army.

Prefently after his coming thither with fome of his Troups, before his whole army was come up, he received intelligence of the *Scots* Armie's near approach, whereupon he fent forth a party of horfe to view them,

who

who found them very ftrong, to the number of
22000 Horfe and Foot well armed and commanded: They marched up towards the Town with fuch
confidence, as if the Gates had been open'd for their
reception; and the General of their Army feem'd to
take no notice of my Lords being in it, for which
afterwards he excufed himfelf; but as they drew near,
they found not fuch entertainment as they expected;
for though they affaulted a Work that was not fi-
nifhed, yet they were beaten off with much lofs.

The Enemy being thus ftopt before the Town,
thought fit to quarter near it, in that part of the
Country; and fo foon as my Lords Army was come
up, he defigned one night to have fallen into their
Quarter; but by reafon of fome neglect of his Orders in not giving timely notice to the party defigned for it, it took not an effect anfwerable to his expectation. In a word, there were three Defigns taken againft the Enemy, whereof if one had but hit,
they would doubtlefs have been loft; but there was
fo much Treachery, Jugling and Falfhood in my
Lord's own Army, that it was impoffible for him
to be fuccefsful in his Defigns and Undertakings.
However, though it failed in the Enemies Foot-
Quarters, which lay neareft the Town; yet it took
good effect in their Horfe-Quarters, which were more
remote; for my Lord's Horfe, Commanded by a
very gallant and worthy Gentleman * falling upon The Lord
                                                  Langdale.
M   them,

them, gave them such an Alarm, that all they could do, was to draw into the Field, where my Lord's Forces charged them, and in a little time routed them totally, and kill'd and took many Prisoners, to the number of 1500.

Upon this the Enemy was forced to draw their whole Army together, and to quarter them a little more remote from the Town, and to seek out inaccessible places for their security, as afterwards appear'd more plainly; for so soon as my Lord had prepared his Army for a March, he drew them forth against the *Scots*, which he found quarter'd upon high Hills close by the River *Tyne*, where they could not be encounter'd but upon very disadvantagious terms; besides, that day proved very stormy and tempestuous, so that my Lord was necessitated to withdraw his Forces, and retire into his own Quarters.

The next day after, the *Scots* Army finding ill harbour in those quarters, marched from hill to hill into another part of the Bishoprick of *Durham*, near the Sea coast, to a Town called *Sunderland*; and thereupon my Lord thought fit to march to *Durham*, to stop their further progress, where he had contrived the business so, that they were either forced to fight or starve within a little time. The first was offered to them twice, that is to say, at *Pensher-hills* one day, and at *Bowden-hills* another day in the Bishoprick of *Durham*:

But

But my Lord found them at both times drawn up in such places, as he could not possibly charge them; wherefore he retired again to *Durham*, with an intention to streighten their Quarters, and to wait upon them, if ever they left their Holds and inaccessible places. In the mean time it hapned that the Earl of *Montross* came to the same place, and having some design for his Majesties service in *Scotland*, desired My Lord to give him the assistance of some of his Forces; and although My Lord stood then in present need of them, and could not coveniently spare any, having so great an Army to oppose; yet out of a desire to advance His Majesties service as much as lay in his power, he was willing to part with 200 Horse and Dragoons to the said Earl.

The *Scots* perceiving My Lords vigilancy and care, contented themselves with their own quarters, which could not have serv'd them long, but that a great misfortune befel My Lords Forces in *York-shire*; for the Governour whom he had left behind with sufficient Forces for the defence of that Country, although he had orders not to encounter the Enemy, but to keep himself in a defensive posture; yet he being a man of great valour and courage, it transported him so much that he resolved to face the Enemy, and offering to keep a Town that was not tenable *, was utterly routed, and *Selby* in *Yorkshire*. himself taken Prisoner, although he fought most gallantly.

So

So foon as my Lord received this fad Intelligence, he upon Confultation, and upon very good Grounds of Reafon, took a refolution not to ftay between the two Armies of the Enemies, *viz.* the *Scots* and the *Englifh*, that had prevailed in *York-fhire*; but immediately to march into *York-fhire* with his Army, to preferve (if poffible) the City of *York* out of the Enemies hands: which retreat was ordered fo well, and with fuch excellent Conduct, that though the Army of the *Scots* marched clofe upon their Rear, and fought them every day of their retreat, yet they gained feveral Paffes for their fecurity, and entred fafe and well into the City of *York*, in *April* 1643.

My Lord being now at *York*, and finding three Armies againft him, *viz.* the Army of the *Scots*, the Army of the *Englifh* that gave the defeat to the Governour of *York*, and an Army that was raifed out of affociate Counties, and but little Ammunition and Provifion in the Town; was forced to fend his Horfe away to quarter in feveral Counties, *viz. Derbyfhire, Nottinghamfhire, Leicefterfhire,* for their fubfiftance, under the Conduct of his Lieutenant-General of the Horfe, My dear Brother Sir *Charles Lucas,* himfelf remaining at *York*, with his Foot and Train for the defence of that City.

In the mean time, the Enemy having clofely befiedged the City on all fides, came to the very Gates thereof, and pull'd out the Earth at one end, as thofe

in

in the City put it in at the other end ; they planted
their great Cannons againſt it, and threw in Grana-
does at pleaſure : But thoſe in the City made ſeveral
ſallies upon them with good ſucceſs.   At laſt, the General of the aſſociate Army of the Enemy, having
cloſely beleaguer'd the North ſide of the Town,
ſprung a Mine under the wall of the Mannor-yard, and
blew part of it up ; and having beaten back the Town-
Forces (although they behaved themſelves very gallantly) enter'd the Mannor-houſe with a great number of their men, which as ſoon as my Lord perceived, he went away in all haſte, even to the amazement
of all that were by, not knowing what he intended to
do ; and drew 80 of his own Regiment of Foot, called the White-Coats, all ſtout and valiant Men, to
that Poſt, who fought the Enemy with that courage,
that within a little time they killed and took 1500 of
them; and My Lord gave preſent order to make up the
breach which they had made in the wall ; Whereupon
the Enemy remain'd without any other attempt in that
kind, ſo long, till almoſt all proviſion for the ſupport
of the ſoldiery in the City was ſpent, which never-
theleſs was ſo well ordered by my Lords Prudence,
that no Famine or great extremity of want en-
ſued.

My Lord having held out in that manner above
two Months, and withſtood the ſtrength of three
Armies ; and ſeeing that his Lieutenant-General of

N   the

the Horſe whom he had ſent for relief to His Majeſty, could not ſo ſoon obtain it (although he uſed
his beſt endeavour) for to gain yet ſome little time,
began to treat with the Enemy; ordering in the mean
while, and upon the Treaty, to double and treble
his Guards. At laſt after three Months time from
the beginning of the Siege, His Majeſty was pleaſed
to ſend an Army, which joining with my Lords Horſe
that were ſent to quarter in the aforeſaid Countreys,
came to relieve the City, under the Conduct of the
moſt Gallant and Heroick Prince *Rupert*, his Ne-
phew; upon whoſe approach near *York*, the Enemy
drew from before the City, into an entire Body, and
marched away on the Weſt-ſide of the River *Owſe*,
that runs through the City, His Majeſties Forces
being then of the Eaſt-ſide of that River.

My Lord immediately ſent ſome perſons of Quality to attend His Highneſs, and to invite him into
the City to conſult with him about that important
Affair, and to gain ſo much time as to open a Port
to march forth with his Cannon and Foot which
were in the Town, to join with His Highneſs's Forces; and went himſelf the next day in perſon to wait
on His Highneſs; where after ſome Conferences, he
declared his Mind to the Prince, deſiring His Highneſs not to attempt any thing as yet upon the Enemy;
for he had intelligence that there was ſome diſcon-
tent between them, and that they were reſolved to
divide

divide themselves, and so to raise the Siege without fighting: Besides, my Lord expected within two dayes, Collonel *Cleavering*, with above three thousand men out of the North, and two thousand drawn out of several Garisons, (who also came at the same time, though it was then too late) But His Highness answered my Lord, That he had a Letter from His Majesty (then at *Oxford*) with a positive and absolute Command to fight the Enemy; which in Obedience, and according to his Duty he was bound to perform. Whereupon my Lord replied, That he was ready and willing for his part, to obey his Highness in all things, no otherwise then if His Majesty was there in Person Himself; and though several of my Lords Friends advised him not to engage in Battel, because the Command (as they said) was taken from Him: Yet my Lord answer'd them, That happen what would, he would not shun to fight, for he had no other ambition but to live and dye a Loyal Subject to His Majesty.

Then the Prince and my Lord conferr'd with several of their Officers, amongst whom there were several Disputes concerning the advantages which the Enemy had of Sun, Wind and Ground. The Horse of His Majesties Forces, was drawn up in both Wings upon that fatal Moor call'd *Hessom-Moor*; and my Lord ask'd His Highness what Service he would be pleas'd to command him; who return'd this Answer,

fwer, That he would begin no action upon the E-
nemy, till early in the morning; defiring my Lord
to repofe himfelf till then: Which my Lord did,
and went to reft in his own Coach that was clofe by
in the Field, until the time appointed.

Not long had My Lord been there, but he heard
a great noife and thunder of fhooting, which gave
him notice of the Armies being engaged: Whereupon he immediately put on his Arms, and was no
fooner got on Horfe-back, but he beheld a dif-
mal fight of the Horfe of His Majefties right Wing,
which out of a panick fear had left the Field, and
run away with all the fpeed they could; and though
my Lord made them ftand once, yet they immediately betook themfelves to their heels again, and
killed even thofe of their own party that endeavoured to ftop them; the Left Wing in the mean time,
Commanded by thofe two Valiant Perfons, the
Lord *Goring*, and Sir *Charles Lucas*, having the better of the Enemies Right Wing, which they beat
back moft valiantly three times, and made their General retreat, in fo much that they founded Victory.

In this Confufion my Lord (accompanied onely
with his Brother Sir *Charles Cavendifh*, Major *Scot*,
Capt. *Mazine*, and his Page) haftning to fee in what
pofture his own Regiment was, met with a Troop
of Gentlemen-Voluntiers, who formerly had chofen

fen him their Captain, notwithftanding he was General of an Army; to whom my Lord fpake after
this manner: *Gentlemen,* faid he, *You have done me the*
Honour to chufe me your Captain, and now is the fitteft
time that I may do you fervice; wherefore if yon'l follow
me, I fhall lead you on the beft I can, and fhew you the
way to your own Honour. They being as glad of my
Lords Profer, as my Lord was of their Readinefs,
went on with the greateft Courage; and paffing
through Two Bodies of Foot, engaged with each
other not at forty yards diftance, received not the
leaft hurt, although they fired quick upon each other;
but marched towards a *Scots* Regiment of Foot,
which they charged and routed; in which Encounter my Lord himfelf kill'd Three with his Pages half-
leaden Sword, for he had no other left him; and
though all the Gentlemen in particular, offer'd him
their Swords, yet my Lord refufed to take a Sword
of any of them. At laft, after they had pafs'd through
this Regiment of Foot, a Pike-man made a ftand to
the whole Troop; and though my Lord charg'd
him twice or thrice, yet he could not enter him;
but the Troop difpatched him foon.

    In all thefe Encounters my Lord got not the leaft
hurt, though feveral were flain about him; and his
White-Coats fhew'd fuch an extraordinary Valour
and Courage in that Action, that they were kill'd in
Rank and File: And here I cannot but mention by

                        the

the way, That it is remarkable, that in all actions and undertakings where My Lord was in Perſon himſelf, he was always Victorious, and proſpered in the execution of his deſigns ; but whatſoever was loſt or ſucceeded ill, happen'd in his abſence, and was cauſed either by the Treachery, or Negligence and Careleſneſs of his Officers.

My Lord being the laſt in the Field, and ſeeing that all was loſt, and that every one of His Majeſties Party made their eſcapes in the beſt manner they could; he being moreover inquired after by ſeveral of his Friends, who had all a great love and reſpect for my Lord, eſpecially by the then Earl of *Craford* (who lov'd my Lord ſo well that he gave 20 s. to one that aſſured him of his being alive and ſafe, telling him, that that was all he had) went towards *York* late at night, accompanied onely with his Brother, and one or two of his ſervants; and coming near the Town, met His Highneſs Prince *Rupert*, with the Lieutenant General of the Army, the Lord *Ethyn* ; His Highneſs asked My Lord how the buſineſs went ? To whom he anſwered, That all was loſt and gone on their ſide.

That night my Lord remained in *York*; and having nothing left in his power to do his Majeſty any further ſervice in that kind ; for he had neither Ammunition, nor Money to raiſe more Forces, to keep either *York*, or any other Towns that were yet in His Majeſties Devotion, well knowing that thoſe
which

which were left could not hold out long, and being also loath to have afperfions caft upon him, that he did fell them to the Enemy, in cafe he could not keep them; he took a Refolution, and that juftly and honourably, to forfake the Kingdom ; and to that end, went the next morning to the Prince, and acquainted him with his Defign, defiring His Highnefs would be pleafed to give this true and juft report of him to his Majefty, that he had behaved himfelf like an honeft man, a Gentleman, and a Loyal fubject : Which requeft the Prince having granted, my Lord took his leave; and being conducted by a Troop of Horfe, and a Troop of Dragoons to *Scarborough*, went to Sea, and took fhipping for *Hamborough* ; the Gentry of the Country, who alfo came to take their leaves of My Lord, being much troubled at his departure, and fpeaking very honourably of him, as furely they had no reafon to the contrary.

THE

The Second Book.

H Aving hitherto faithfully related the life of My Noble Lord and Husband, and the chief Acti- ons which He performed during the time of his being employed in His Majesties Service for the Good and Interest of his King and Country, until the time of his going out of *England,* I shall now give you a just ac- count of all that passed during the time of his banish- ment, till the return into his native Country.

My Lord being a Wise Man, and foreseeing well what the loss of that fatal Battle upon *Hessom-moor,* near *York,* would produce, by which not onely those of His Majesties Party in the Northern parts of the Kingdom, but in all other parts of His Majesties Do- minions both in *England, Scotland* and *Ireland* were lost and undone, and that there was no other way, but either to quit the Kingdom, or submit to the Enemy, or die; he resolved upon the former, and preparing for his journey, asked his Steward, How Much Money he had left? Who answer'd, That he had but 90 l. My Lord not being at all startled at so small a Summ, although his present design required much more, was resolved too seek his Fortune, even with that litle; and thereupon having taken leave of His Highness Prince *Rupert,* and the rest that were pre-
                                                           sent,

fent, went to *Scarborough* (as before is mentioned) where two Ships were prepared for *Hamborough* to fet fail within 24 hours, in which he embarqued with his Company, and arrived in four days time to the faid City, which was on the *8th* of *July*, 1644.

In one of thefe Ships was my Lord, with his two Sons, *Charles* Vifcount *Mansfield*, and Lord *Henry Cavendifh*, now Earl of *Ogle*; as alfo Sir *Charles Cavendifh*, My Lord's Brother; the then Lord Bifhop of *London-derry* Dr. *Bramhall*; the Lord *Falconbridg*, the Lord *Widdrington*, Sir *William Carnaby*, who after died at *Paris*, and his Brother Mr. *Francis Carnaby*, who went prefently in the fame Ship back again for *England*, and foon after was flain by the Enemy, near *Sherborne* in *York-fhire*, befides many of my Lord's and their fervants : In the other Ship was the Earl of *Ethyne*, Lieutenant General of My Lord's Army, and the Lord *Cornworth*. But before My Lord landed at *Hamborough*, his eldeft Son *Charles*, Lord *Mansfield*, fell fick of the Small-Pox, and not long after his younger Son *Henry*, now Earl of *Ogle*, fell likewife dangeroufly ill of the Meafels ; but it pleafed God that they both happily recovered.

My Lord finding his Company and Charge very great, although he fent feveral of his Servants back again into *England*; and having no means left to maintain him, was forced to feek for Credit ; where at laft he got fo much as would in part relieve his necef-

P   fities :

ſities; and whereas heretofore he had been contented, for want of a Coach, to make uſe of a Waggon, when his occaſions drew him abroad; he was now able (with the credit he had got) to buy a Coach and nine Horſes of an *Holſatian* breed; for which Horſes he paid 160 l. and was afterwards offer'd for one of them an hundred Piſtols at *Paris*; but he re-fuſed the money, and preſented ſeven of them to Her Majeſty the Queen-Mother of *England*, and kept two for his own uſe.

After my Lord had ſtay'd in *Hamborough* from *July* 1644, till *February* 164$\frac{5}{4}$, he being reſolved to go into *France*, went by Sea from *Hamborough* to *Amſterdam*, and from thence to *Rotterdam*, where he ſent one of his Servants with a Complement and tender of his humble Service to Her Highneſs the then Princeſs Royal, the Queen of *Bohemia*, the Princeſs Dowager of *Orange*, and the Prince of *Orange*, which was received with much kindneſs and civility.

From *Rotterdam* he directed his Journey to *Antwerp*, and from thence with one Coach, one Cha-riot, and two Waggons, he went to *Mechlin* and *Bruſſels*, where he received a Viſit from the Gover-nour, the Marqueſs of *Caſtel Rodrigo*, the Duke of *Lorrain*, and Count *Piccolomini*.

From thence he ſet forth for *Valenchin* and *Cambray*, where the Governour of the Town, uſed my Lord with great reſpect and civility, and deſired him

to

to give the word that night. Thence he went to *Pe-roon*, a Frontier Town in *France*, (where the Vice-Governour in abfence of the Governour of that place, did likewife entertain my Lord with all re-fpect, and defired him to give the Word that night) and fo to *Paris* without any further ftay.

My Lord being arrived at *Paris*, which was in *A-pril* 1645, immediately went to tender his humble du-ty to Her Majefty the Queen-Mother of *England*, where it was my Fortune to fee him the firft time, I being then one of the Maids of Honour to Her Majefty; and after he had ftay'd there fome time, he was pleafed to take fome particular notice of me, and exprefs more then an ordinary affection for me; infomuch that he refolved to chufe me for his Se-cond Wife; for he having but two *Sons*, purpofed to marry me, a young Woman, that might prove fruitful to him, and encreafe his Pofterity by a Ma-fculine Off-fpring: Nay, He was fo defirous of Male-Iffue, that I have heard him fay, He cared not, (fo God would be pleafed to give him many Sons) although they came to be Perfons of the meaneft Fortunes; but God (it feems) had ordered it otherwife, and fruftrated his Defigns, by making me barren, which yet did never leffen his Love and Affection for me.

After My Lord was married, having no Eftate or Means left him to maintain himfelf and his Family, he

he was necessitated to seek for Credit, and live upon the
Courtesie of those that were pleased to Trust him;
which although they did for some while, and shew'd
themselves very civil to My Lord, yet they grew wea-
ry at length, insomuch that his Steward was forced one
time to tell him, That he was not able to provide a
Dinner for him, for his Creditors were resolved to
trust him no longer. My Lord being always a great
master of his Passions, was, at least shew'd himself not
in any manner troubled at it, but in a pleasant humour told me, that I must of necessity pawn my
Cloaths, to make so much Money as would procure
a Dinner. I answer'd, That my Cloaths would be
but of small value, and therefore desired my Waiting-
Maid* to pawn some small toys, which I had formerly
given her, which she willingly did. The same day in
the afternoon, My Lord spake himself to his Creditors, and both by his civil Deportment, and persuasive
Arguments, obtained so much, that they did not onely trust him for more necessaries, but lent him Mony
besides, to redeem those Toys that were pawned.
Hereupon I sent my Waiting-Maid into *England,* to
my Brother the Lord *Lucas,* for that small Portion
which was left me, and my Lord also immediately
after dispatched one of his Servants*, who was then
Governour to his Sons, to some of his Friends, to
try what means he could procure for his subsistance;
but though he used all the industry and endeavour he
                                                could,

Mrs. *Chap-
lain*, now
Mrs. *Top.*

Mr. *Beno-
ist.*

could, yet he effected but little, by reason every body
was so affraid of the Parliament, that they durst not
relieve Him, who was counted a Traitor for his Honest
and Loyal service to his King and Country.

Not long after, My Lord had profers made him
of some Rich Matches in *England* for his two Sons,
whom therefore he sent thither with one Mr. *Loving*,
hoping by that means to provide both for them and
himself ; but they being arrived there, out of some
reasons best known to them, declared their unwilling-
ness to Marry as yet, continuing nevertheless in *England*, and living as well as they could.

Some two years after my Lord's Marriage, when
he had prevailed so far with his Creditors, that they
began to trust him anew ; the first thing he did was,
that he removed out of those Lodgings in *Paris*, where
he had been necessitated to live hitherto, to a House
which he hired for himself and his Family, and furnish-
ed it as well as his new gotten Credit would permit ;
and withal, resolving for his own recreation and diver-
tisement in his banished condition, to exercise the Art
of Mannage, which he is a great lover and Master of,
bought a Barbary-horse for that purpose, which cost
him 200 Pistols, and soon after, another Barbary-
horse from the Lord *Crofts*, for which he was to pay
him 100 l. when he returned into *England*.

About this time, there was a Council call'd at
St. *Germain*, in which were present, besides My Lord,

Q   Her

Her Majesty the now Queen Mother of *England*; His Highness the Prince, our now gracious King; His Cousin Prince *Rupert*; the Marquess of *Worcester*, the then Marquess, now Duke of *Ormond*, the Lord *Jermyn* now Earl of St. *Albans*, and several others; where after several debates concerning the then present condition of His Majesty King *Charles* the First, my Lord delivered his sentiment, that he could perceive no other probability of procuring Forces for His Majesty, but an assistance of the *Scots*; But Her Majesty was pleased to answer my Lord, That he was too quick.

Not long after, When my Lord had begun to settle himsef in his mentioned new house, His gracious Master the Prince, having taken a resolution to go into *Holland* upon some designs; Her Majesty the Queen Mother desired my Lord to follow him, promising to engage for his debts which hitherto he had contracted at *Paris*, and commanding Her Controller * and Treasurer * to be bound for them in Her behalf; which they did, although the Creditors would not content themselves, until my Lord had joined his word to theirs; So great and generous was the bounty and favour of Her Majesty to my Lord! considering she had already given him heretofore near upon 2000 l. *Sterling*, even at that time when Her Majesty stood most in need of it.

Sir *Henry Wood.*
Sir —— *Foster.*

My

My Lord, after his Highnefs the Prince was gone,
being ready to execute Her Majefties Commands in
following Him, and preparing for his Journey, wanted the chief thing, which was Money; and having
much endeavoured for it, at laft had the good Fortune to obtain upon Credit three or four hundred
pounds *fterl.* With which Sum he fet out of *Paris* in
the fame Equipage he entred, *viz.* One Coach, which
he had newly caufed to be made, (wherein were the
Lord *Widdrington*, my Lord's Brother Sir *Charles
Cavendifh*, Mr. *Loving*, my Waiting-Maid, and
fome others, whereof the two later were then returned out of *England*) one little Chariot, that would
onely hold my Lord and my felf; and three Waggons, befides an indifferent number of Servants on
Horfe-back.

That day when we left *Paris*, the Creditors coming to take their Farwell of my Lord, exprefled fo
great a love and kindnefs for him, accompanied
vvith fo many hearty Prayers and Wifhes, that he
could not but profper on his Journey.

Being come into the King of *Spain's* Dominions,
my Lord found a very Noble Reception. At *Cambray* the Governour vvas fo civil, that my Lord coming to that place fomevvhat late; and vvhen it vvas
dark, he commanded fome Lights and Torches to
meet my Lord, and conduct him to his Lodgings:
He offer'd my Lord the Keys of the City, and de-

fir'd

fir'd him to give the Word that night, and moreover invited him to an Entertainment, which he had
made for him of purpose; but it being late, my
Lord (tyred with his Journey) excused himself as civilly as he could; the Governour notwithstanding
being pleased to send all manner of Provisions to my
Lords Lodgings, and charging our Landlord to take
no pay for any thing we had: Which extraordinary
Civilities shewed that he was a Right Noble *Spani-
ard.*

    The next morning early, my Lord went on his
Journey, and was very civilly used in every place of
His Majesty of *Spain*'s Dominions, where he arrived: At last coming to *Antwerp*, He took water to *Rotterdam* (which Town he chose for his
residing place, during the time of his stay in *Holland*) and sent thither to a Friend of his *, a Gentleman of Quality, to provide him some Lodgings;
which he did, and procured them at the house of
one Mrs. B⸺ *ynham*, Widow to an English Merchant,
who had always been very Loyal to His Majesty the
King of *England*, and serviceable to His Majesties
faithful Subjects in whatsoever lay in his Power.

    My Lord being come to *Rotterdam*, was inform-
ed that His Highness the Prince (now our Gracious
King) was gone to Sea: Wherefore he resolved to
follow him, and for that purpose hired a Boat, and
victual'd it; but since no body knew whither His
High-

Sir *William Throckmor-ton,* Knight.

Highnefs was gone; and I being unwilling that my
Lord fhould venture upon fo uncertain a Voyage, and
(as the Proverb is) *Seek a Needle in a Bottle of Hay*,
he defifted from that defign: The Lord *Widdrington*
neverthelefs, and Sir *Will. Throckmorton*, being refolved to find out the Prince, but having by a ftorm
been driven towards the Coaft of *Scotland*, and en-
dangered their lives, they returned without obtaining
their aim.

After fome little time, my Lord having notice
that the Prince was arrived at the *Hague*, he went
to wait on His Highnefs (which he alfo did afterwards
at feveral times, fo long as His Highnefs continued there) expecting fome opportunity where he might
be able to fhew his readinefs to ferve His King and
Countrey, as certainly there was no little hopes for
it; for firft, it was believed that the Englifh Fleet would
come and render it felf into the obedience of the
Prince; next, it was reported that the Duke of *Hamilton* was going out of *Scotland* with a great Army,
into *England*, to the affiftance of His Majefty, and
that His Majefty had then fome party at *Colchefter*;
but it pleafed God that none of thefe proved effectual: For the Fleet did not come in; the Duke of
Hamilton's Army was deftroyed, and *Colchefter* was
taken by the Enemy, where my dear Brother Sir
Charles Lucas, and his dear Friend Sir *George Lile*,
were moft inhumanly murther'd and fhot to death,

R   they

they being both Valiant and Heroick Perſons, good
Soldiers, and moſt Loyal Subjects to His Majeſty;
the one an excellent Commander of Horſe, the o-
ther of Foot.

My Lord having now lived in *Rotterdam* almoſt
ſix months, at a great charge, keeping an open and
noble Table for all comers, and being pleaſed eſpecially to entertain ſuch as were excellent Soldiers, and
noted Commanders of War, whoſe kindneſs he took
as a great Obligation, ſtill hoping that ſome occaſi-
on would happen to invite thoſe worthy Perſons into *England* to ſerve His Majeſty; but ſeeing no probability of either returning into *England*, or doing
His Majeſty any ſervice in that kind, he reſolved to
retire to ſome place where he might live privately;
and having choſen the City of *Antwerp* for that purpoſe, went to the *Hague* to take his leave of His
Highneſs the Prince, our now gracious Soveraign.
My Lord had then but a ſmall ſtock of money left;
for though the then *Marqueſs* of *Hereford* (after
Duke of *Somerſet*, and his Couſin-German, once
removed, the now Earl of *Devonſhire* had lent him
2000 l. between them; yet all that was ſpent, and
above 1000 l. more, which my Lord borrowed during the time he lived in *Rotterdam*, his Expence being the more, by reaſon (as I mentioned) he lived
freely and nobly.

However my Lord, notwithſtanding that little
provi-

provision of Money he had, set forth from *Rotterdam* to *Antwerp*, where for some time he lay in a publick Inne, until one of his Friends that had a great love and respect for my Lord, Mr. *Endymion Porter*, who was Groom of the Bed-chamber to His Majesty King *Charles* the First (a place not onely honourable, but very profitable) being not willing that a Person of such Quality as my Lord, should lie in a publick House, profer'd him Lodgings at the House where he was, and would not let my Lord be at quiet, until he had accepted of them.

My Lord after he had stay'd some while there, endeavouring to find out a House for himself which might fit him and his small Family, (for at that time he had put off most of his Train) and also be for his own content, lighted on one that belonged to the Widow of a famous Picture-drawer, *Van Ruben*, which he took.

About this time my Lord was much necessitated for Money, which forced him to try several ways for to obtain so much as would relieve his present wants. At last Mr. *Alesbury*, the onely Son to Sir *Th. Alesbury*, Knight and Baronet, and Brother to the now Countess of *Clarendon*, a very worthy Gentleman, and great Friend to my Lord, having some Moneys that belonged to the now Duke of *Buckingham*, and seeing my Lord in so great distress, did him the favour

to

to lend him 200 l. (which money my Lord since his return hath honestly and justly repai'd) This relief came so seasonably, that it got my Lord Credit in the City of *Antwerp*, whereas otherwise he would have lost himself to his great disadvantage ; for my Lord having hired the house aforementioned, and wanting Furniture for it, was credited by the Citizens for as many Goods as he was pleased to have, as also for *Meat* and Drink, and all kind of necessaries and provisions, which certainly was a special Blessing of God, he being not onely a stranger in that Nation, but to all appearance, a Ruined man.

After my Lord had been in *Antwerp* sometime, where he lived as retiredly as it was possible for him to do, he gained much love and respect of all that knew or had any business with him : At the beginning of our coming thither, we found but few English (except those that were Merchants) but afterwards their number increased much, especially of Persons of Quality ; and whereas at first there were no more but four Coaches that went the *Tour*, *viz.* the Governors of the Castle, my Lords, and two more, they amounted to the number of above a hundred , before we went from thence ; for all those that had sufficient means, and could go to the price, kept Coaches, and went the *Tour* for their own pleasure. And certainly I cannot in duty and conscience but give this Publick Testimony to that place, That whereas I have observ'd,

ferv'd, that moſt commonly ſuch Towns or Cities
where the Prince of that Country doth not reſide himſelf, or where there is no great reſort of the chief Nobility and Gentry, are but little civiliſed; Certainly
the Inhabitants of the ſaid City of *Antwerp* are the ci-
vileſt, and beſt behaved People that ever I ſaw; ſo
that my Lord lived there with as much content as a
man of his condition could do, and his chief paſtime
and divertiſement conſiſted in the Mannage of the two
afore mentioned Horſes; which he had not enjoyed
long, but the *Barbary*-horſe, for which he paid 200
Piſtols in *Paris*, died, and ſoon after the Horſe which
he had from the Lord *Crofts*; and though he wanted
preſent means to repair theſe his loſſes, yet he endeavoured and obtained ſo much Credit at laſt, that he
was able to buy two others, and by degrees ſo many
as amounted in all to the number of 8. In which he
took ſo much delight and pleaſure, that though he was
then in diſtreſs for Money, yet he would ſooner have
tried all other ways, then parted with any of them;
for I have hear'd him ſay, that good Horſes are ſo rare,
as not to be valued for Mony, and that He who would
buy him out of his Pleaſure, (meaning his Horſes)
muſt pay dear for it. For inſtance I ſhall mention ſome
paſſages which happen'd when My Lord was in *Antwerp.*

First; A ſtranger coming thither, and ſeeing my
Lords Horſes, had a great mind to buy one of them,

S   which

which my Lord loved above the reſt, and called him
his Favourite, a fine *Spaniſh* Horſe; intreating my
Lords Eſcuyer to acquaint him with his deſire, and
ask the price of the ſaid Horſe: My Lord, when he
heard of it, commanded his Servant, that if the Chapman returned, he ſhould be brought before him; which
being done accordingly, my Lord asked him, whether
he was reſolved to buy his *Spaniſh* Horſe? Yes, anſwered he, my Lord, and I'le give your Lordſhip a
good price for him. I make no doubt of it, replied My
Lord, or elſe you ſhall not have him: But you muſt
know, ſaid he, that the price of that Horſe is 1000 l.
to day, to morrow it will be 2000 l. next day 3000 l.
and ſo forth. By which the Chapman perceiving
that my Lord was unwilling to part with the ſaid Horſe
for any Money, took his leave, and ſo went his
ways.

The next was, That the Duke *de Guiſe*, who was
alſo a great lover of good Horſes, hearing much Com-
mendation of a gray leaping Horſe, which my Lord
then had, told the Gentleman that praiſed and commended him, That if my Lord was willing to ſell
the ſaid Horſe, he would give 600 Piſtols for him.
The Gentleman knowing my Lords humour, anſwered again, That he was confident, my Lord would
never part with him for any mony, and to that purpoſe ſent a Letter to my Lord from *Paris*; but my
Lord was ſo far from ſelling that Horſe, that he was
                                        diſpleaſed

difpleafed to hear that any Price fhould be offer'd
for him: So great a Love hath my Lord for good
Horfes! And certainly I have obferved, and do verily believe, that fome of them had alfo a particular Love to my Lord; for they feemed to rejoice
whenfoever he came into the Stables, by their
trampling action, and the noife they made; nay,
they would go much better in the Mannage, when
my Lord was by, then when he was abfent; and
when he rid them himfelf, they feemed to take much
pleafure and pride in it. But of all forts of Horfes,
my Lord loved *Spanifh* Horfes and *Barbes* beft; faying, That *Spanifh* Horfes were like Princes, and
Barbes like Gentlemen, in their kind. And this
was the chief Recreation and Paftime my Lord had
in *Antwerp*.

I will now return to my former Difcourfe, and
the Relation of fome Important Affairs and Actions which happen'd about this time: His Majefty
(our now Gracious King, *Charles* the Second) fome
time after he was gone out of *Holland*, and returned into *France*, took his Journey from thence to *Breda*
(if I remember well) to treat there with his Subjects of *Scotland*, who had then made fome offers of
Agreement: My Lord, according to his duty, went
thither to wait on His Majefty, and was there in
Council with His Majefty, His Highnefs the then
Prince of *Orange*, His Majefties Brother-in-law, and
                                              fome

some other Privy-Counsellors; in which, after several Debates concerning that Important Affair, His
Highness the Prince of *Orange*, and my Lord, agreed
in one Opinion, *viz*. That they could perceive no
other and better way at that present for His Majesty, but to make an Agreement with His Subjects
of *Scotland*, upon any Condition, and to go into
Scotland in Person Himself, that he might but be
sure of an Army, there being no probability or
appearance then of getting an Army any where else.
Which Counsel, either out of the then alledged Reasons, or some others best known to His Majesty,
was embraced; His Majesty agreeing with the *Scots*
so far, (notwithstanding they were so unreasonable
in their Treaty, that His Majesty had hardly Patience to hear them) that he resolved to go into *Scotland* in Person; and though my Lord had an earnest
desire to wait on His Majesty thither, yet the *Scots*
would not suffer him to come, or be in any part of
that Kingdom: Wherefore out of his Loyalty and
Duty, he gave His Majesty the best advice he could,
viz. that he conceived it most safe for His Majesty
to adhere to the Earl of *Argyle's* Party, which he
supposed to be the strongest; but especially, to recon-
cile *Hamilton's* and *Argyle's* Party, and compose the
differences between them; for then His Majesty would
be sure of Two Parties, whereas otherwise He would
leave an Enemy behind Him, which might cause
His

His overthrow, and endanger His Majesties Person; and if His Majesty could but get the Power into his own hands, he might do hereafter what he pleased.

His Majesty being arrived in *Scotland*, ordered his affairs so wisely, that soon after he got an Army to march with him into *England*; but whether they were all Loyal, is not for me to dispute: However *Argyle* was discontented, as it appear'd by two complaining Letters he sent to my Lord, which my Lord gave His Majesty notice of; so that onely the Duke of *Hamilton* went with His Majesty, who fought and died like a Valiant Man, and a Loyal subject. In this fight between the *English* and *Scots*, His Majesty expressed an extraordinary Courage ; and though his Army was in a manner destroyed, yet the Glory of an Heroick Prince remained with our gracious Soveraign.

In the mean time, whilest His Majesty was yet in *Scotland*, and before he marched with His Army into *England*, it happen'd that the Elector of *Brandenburg*, and Duke of *Newburg*, upon some differences, having raised Forces against each other, but afterwards concluded a Peace between them , were pleased to profer those Forces to my Lord for His Majesties use and service, which (as the Lord Chancellour, who was then in *France*, sent word to my Lord) was the onely Foreign profer that had been made to his Majesty. My Lord immediately gave His Majesty notice of it; but whether it was for want of convenient Transporta-

T   tion,

tion, or Mony, or that the *Scots* did not like the affiftance, that profer was not accepted.

Concerning the affairs and intrigues that pafs'd in
Scotland, and *England,* during the time of His Majefties ftay there, I am ignorant of them; neither doth
it belong to me now to write, or give an account of a-
ny thing elfe but what concerns the Hiftory of my Noble Lord and Husbands Life, and his own Actions;
who fo foon as he had Intelligence that the *Scottifh* Army, which went with His Majefty into *England,* was
defeated, and that no body knew what was become
of His Majefty, fell into fo violent a Paffion, that I
verily believed it would have endanger'd his life; but
when afterwards the happy news came of His Maje-
jefties fafe arrival in *France,* never any Subject could
rejoice more then my Lord did.

About this time it chanced, that my Lords Brother
Sir *Charles Cavendifh,* and my felf, took a journey into
England, occafioned both by my Lord's extream want
and neceffity, and his Bothers Eftate; which having
been under Sequeftration from the time (or foon after) he went out of *England,* was then, in cafe he did
not return and compound for it, to be fold out-right;
Sir *Charles* was unwilling to receive his Eftate upon
fuch conditions, and would rather have loft it, then compounded for it: But my Lord confidering it was better to recover fomething, then lofe all, intreated the
Lord Chancellour, who was then in *Antwerp,* to perfwade

fwade his Brother to a compofition, which his Lordfhip did very effectually, and proved himfelf a Noble
and true Friend in it.   We had fo fmall a Provifion
of money when we fet forth our Journey for *Eng-*
land, that it was hardly able to carry us to *London*,
but were forced to ftay at *Southwark*; where Sir
Charles fent into *London* for one that had formerly
been his Steward; and having declared to him his
wants and neceffities, defir'd him to try his Credit.
He feemed ready to do his Mafter what fervice he could
in that kind; but pretending withall, that his Credit
was but fmall, Sir *Charles* gave him his Watch to
pawn, and with that money paid thofe fmall fcores
we had made in our Lodging there.   From thence we
went to fome other Lodgings that were prepared for
us in *Covent-Garden*; and having refted our felves
fome time, I defired my Brother the Lord *Lucas*, to
claim, in my behalf, fome fubfiftance for my felf out
of my Lords Eftate, (for it was declared by the
Parliament, That the Lands of thofe that were banifhed, fhould be fold to any that would buy them,
onely their Wives and Children were allowed to put
in their Claims:) But he received this Anfwer, That
I could not expect the leaft allowance, by reafon
my Lord and Husband had been the greateft Traitor
of *England* (that is to fay, the honefteft man, becaufe
he had been moft againft them.)

Then Sir *Charles* intrufted fome perfons to compound

pound for his Eftate; but it being a good while before they agreed in their Compofition, and then before the Rents could be received, we having in the
mean time nothing to live on, muft of neceffity have
been ftarved, had not Sir *Charles* got fome Credit
of feveral Perfons, and that not without great difficulty; for all thofe that had Eftates, were afraid to
come near him, much lefs to affift him, until he was
fure of his own Eftate. So much is Mifery and Poverty fhun'd!

But though our Condition was hard, yet my dear
Lord and Husband, whom we left in *Antwerp*, was
then in a far greater diftrefs then our felves; for at
our departure he had nothing but what his Credit
was able to procure him; and having run upon the
fcore fo long without paying any the leaft part thereof, his Creditors began to grow impatient, and refolved to truft him no longer: Wherefore he fent
me word, That if his Brother did not prefently relieve him, he was forced to ftarve. Which doleful
news caufed great fadnefs and melancholy in us both,
and withal made his Brother try his utmoft endeavour
to procure what moneys he could for his fubfiftance,
who at laft got 200 l. *fterl.* upon Credit, which he immediately made over to my Lord.

But in the mean time, before the faid money could
come to his hands, my Lord had been forced to fend
for all his Creditors, and declare to them his great wants
and

and neceffities; where his Speech was fo effectual, and
made fuch an impreffion in them, that they had all
a deep fenfe of my Lords Misfortunes; and inftead
of urging the payment of his Debts, promifed him,
That he fhould not want any thing in whatfoever
they were able to affift him; which they alfo very
nobly and civilly performed, furnifhing him with all
manner of provifions and neceffaries for his further
fubfiftance; fo that my Lord was then in a much
better condition amongft ftrangers, then we in our
Native Countrey.

At laft when Sir *Charles Cavendifh* had compounded for his Eftate, and agreed to pay 4500 l. for
it, the Parliament caufed it again to be furvey-
ed, and made him pay 500 l. more, which was
more then many others had paid for much greater
Eftates; fo that Sir *Charles* to pay this Compofition, and difcharge fome Debts, was neceffitated to
fell fome Land of his at an under-rate. My Lords
two Sons (who were alfo in *England* at that time)
were no lefs in want and neceffity, then we, having
nothing but bare Credit to live on; and my Lords
Eftate being then to be fold outright, Sir *Charles*, his
Brother, endeavoured, if poffible, to fave the two
chief Houfes, *viz. Welbeck* and *Bolfover*, being refolved rather to part with fome more of his Land,
which he had lately compounded for, then to let
them fall into the Enemies hands; but before fuch

U   time

time as he could compafs the money, fome body had bought *Bolfover*, with an intention to pull it down, and make money of the Materials; of whom Sir *Charles* was forced to buy it again at a far greater Rate then he might have had it at firft, notwithftanding a great part of it was pulled down already; and though my Lords eldeft Son *Charles* Lord *Mansfield*, had thofe mentioned Houfes fome time in pof-feffion, after the death of his Uncle; yet for want of Means he was not able to repair them.

I having now been in *England* a year and a half, fome Intelligence which I received of my Lords being not very well, and the fmall hopes I had of getting fome relief out of his Eftate, put me upon defign of returning to *Antwerp* to my Lord; and Sir *Charles*, his Brother, took the fame refolution, but was prevented by an Ague that feized upon him. Not long had I been with my Lord, but we received the fad news of his Brothers death, which was an extream afflidion both to my Lord, and my felf, for they loved each other entirely: In truth, He was a Perfon of fo great worth, fuch extraordinary civili-ty, fo obliging a Nature, fo full of Generofity, Juftice and Charity, befides all manner of Learning, efpecially in the *Mathematicks*, that not onely his Friends, but even his Enemies, did much lament his lofs.

After my return out of *England*, to my Lord, the
Credi-

Creditors suppofing I had brought great ftore of money along with me, came all to my Lord to foli-
cite the payment of their Debts; but when my Lord
had informed them of the truth of the bufinefs, and
defired their patience fomewhat longer, with affu-
rance that fo foon as he received any money, he
would honeftly and juftly fatisfie them, they were
not onely willing to forbear the payment of thofe
Debts he had contracted hitherto, but to credit him
for the future, and fupply him with fuch Neceffaries as he fhould defire of them. And this was the
onely happinefs which my Lord had in his diftreffed
condition, and the chief bleffing of the Eternal and
Merciful God, in whofe Power are all things, who
ruled the hearts and minds of men, and filled them
with Charity and Compaffion; for certainly it was
a work of Divine Providence, that they fhewed fo
much love, refpect and honour to my Lord, a ftran-
ger to their Nation; and notwithftanding his ruined
Condition, and the fmall appearance of recovering
his own, credited him wherefoever he lived, both in
France, *Holland*, *Brabant* and *Germany*; that although my Lord was banifhed his Native Countrey,
and difpoffeffed from his own Eftate, could neverthelefs live in fo much Splendor and Grandure as he
did.

In this Condition (and how little foever the appearance was) my Lord was never without hopes of

feeing

seeing yet (before his death) a happy iſſue of all his misfortunes and ſufferings, eſpecially of the Reſtauration of His moſt Gracious King and Maſter, to His Throne and Kingly Rights, whereof he always had aſſured Hopes, well knowing, that it was impoſſible for the Kingdom to ſubſiſt long under ſo many changes of Government; and whenſoever I expreſſed how little faith I had in it, he would gently reprove me, ſaying, I believ'd leaſt, what I deſir'd moſt; and could never be happy if I endeavour'd to exclude all hopes, and entertain'd nothing but doubts and fears.

The City of *Antwerp* in which we lived, being a place of great reſort for Strangers and Travellers, His Majeſty (our now gracious King, *Charles* the Second) paſſed thorough it, when he went his Journey towards *Germany*; and after my Lord had done his humble duty, and waited on His Majeſty, He was pleaſed to Honour him with His Preſence at his Houſe. The ſame did almoſt all ſtrangers that were Perſons of Quality; if they made any ſtay in the Town, they would come and viſit my Lord, and ſee the Mannage of his Horſes: And, amongſt the reſt, the Duke of *Oldenburg*, and the Prince of *Eaſt-Frieſland*, did my Lord the Honour, and preſented him with Horſes of their own breed.

One time it happen'd, that His Highneſs *Dom John d' Auſtria* (who was then Governour of thoſe Provinces)

came

came to *Antwerp*, and stayed there some few days; and
then almost all his Court waited on my Lord, so that
one day I reckoned about seventeen Coaches, in
which were all Persons of Quality, who came in
the morning of purpose to see my Lord's Mannage;
My Lord receiving so great an honour thought
it fit to shew his respect and civility to them, and
to ride some of his Horses himself, which otherwise
he never did but for his own excercise and delight. A-
mongst the rest of those great and noble Persons, there
were two of our Nation, *viz.* the then Marquess, now
Duke of *Ormond*, and the Earl of *Bristol*; but *Dom
John* was not there in Person, excusing himself afterwards to my Lord (when my Lord waited on him)
that the multiplicity of his weighty affairs had hindred
his coming thither, which my Lord accounted as a very high honour and favour from so great a Prince; and
conceiving it his duty to wait on his Highness, but
being unknown to him, the Earl of *Bristol*, who had
acquaintance with him, did my Lord the favour, and
upon his request, presented him to his Highness; which
favour of the said Earl my Lord highly resented.

   Dom John received my Lord with all kindness and
respect; for although there were many great and noble
Persons that waited on him in an out room, yet so
soon as his Highness heard of my Lord's, and the Earl
of *Bristol's* being there, he was pleased to admit them
before all the rest. My Lord, after he had passed his

X   Complements,

Complements, told His Highnefs, That he found himfelf bound in all duty, to make his humble acknowledgments for the Favour he received from His Catholick Majefty, for permitting and fuffering him (a banifhed man) to live in His Dominions, and under the Government of His Highnefs; whereupon *Dom John* ask'd my Lord whether he wanted any thing, and whether he liv'd peaceably without any moleftation or difturbance? My Lord anfwer'd, That he lived as much to his own content, as a banifh'd man could do; and received more refpect and civility from that City, then he could have expected; for which he returned his moft humble thanks to his Catholick Majefty, and His Highnefs. After fome fhort Difcourfe, my Lord took his leave of *Dom John*; Several of the *Spaniards* advifing him to go into *Spain*, and affuring him of His Catholick Majefties Kindnefs and Favour; but my Lord being engaged in the City of *Antwerp*, and befides, in years, and wanting means for fo long and chargeable a voyage, was not able to embrace their motions; and furely he was fo well pleafed with the great Civilities he received from that City, that then he was refolved to chufe no other refiding place all the time of his banifhment, but that; he being not onely credited there for all manner of Provifions and Neceffaries for his fubfiftance, but alfo free both from ordinary and extraordinary Taxes, and from paying Excife,

which

which was a great favour and obligation to my Lord.

After His Highnefs *Dom John* had left the Government of thofe Provinces, the Marquefs of *Caracena* fucceeded in his place, who having a great defire to fee my Lord ride in the Mannage, entreated a Gentleman of the City, that was acquainted with my Lord, to beg that favour of him. My Lord having not been at that Exercife fix weeks, or two months, by reafon of fome ficknefs that made him unfit for it, civilly begg'd his excufe; but he was fo much importuned by the faid Gentleman, that at laft he granted his Requeft, and rid one or two Horfes in prefence of the faid Marquefs of *Caracena*, and the then Marquefs, now Duke of *Ormond*, who often ufed to honour my Lord with his Company: The faid Marquefs of *Caracena* feem'd to take much pleafure and fatisfaction in it, and highly complemented my Lord; and certainly I have obferved, That Noble and Meritorious perfons take great delight in honouring each other.

But not onely ftrangers, but His Majefty Himfelf (our now Gracious Soveraign) was pleafed to fee my Lord ride, and one time did ride Himfelf, He being an Excellent Mafter of that Art, and inftructed by my Lord, who had the Honour to fet Him firft on a Horfe of Mannage, when he was His Governour; where His Majefties Capacity was fuch, that being but Ten years of Age, he

would

would ride leaping Horſes, and ſuch as would overthrow others, and mannage them with the greateſt
Skill and Dexterity, to the admiration of all that
beheld Him.

Nor was this the onely Honour my Lord received
from His Majeſty, but His Majeſty and all the Royal Race; that is to ſay, Her Highneſs the then Princeſs Royal, His Highneſs the Duke of *York*, with
His Brother the Duke of *Glocester*, (except
the Princeſſe *Henrietta*, now Ducheſs of *Orle-
ans*) being met one time in *Antwerp*, were pleaſed
to honour my Lord with their Preſence, and accept
of a ſmall Entertainment at his Houſe, ſuch as his
preſent Condition was able to afford them. And ſome
other time His Majeſty paſſing through the City, was
pleaſed to accept of a private Dinner at my Lord's
Houſe; after which I receiving that gracious Favour
from His Majeſty, that he was pleaſed to ſee me, he
did merrily, and in jeſt, tell me, *That he perceived
my Lord's Credit could procure better Meat then His own*;
Again, ſome other time, upon a merry Challenge playing a Game at Butts with my Lord, (when my Lord
had the better of Him) *What (ſaid He) my Lord,
have you invited me, to play the Rook with me?* Although their Stakes were not at all conſiderable, but
onely for Paſtime.

These paſſages I mention onely to declare my Lord's
happineſs in his miſeries, which he received by the honour

nour and kindneſs not onely of foreign Princes, but
of his own Maſter, and Gracious Soveraign: I will not
now ſpeak of the good eſteem his late Majeſty
King *Charles* the Firſt, and Her Majeſty the now
Queen-Mother, had of him, who always held and
found him a very loyal and faithful Subject, although
Fortune was pleaſed to oppoſe him in the height of his
endeavours; for his onely and chief intention was to
hinder His Majeſties Enemies from executing that
cruel deſign which they had upon their gracious and
merciful King; In which he tried his uttermoſt power,
in ſo much, that I have heard him ſay out of a paſſio-
nate Zeal and Loyalty, That he would willingly ſacrifice himſelf, and all his Poſterity, for the ſake of his
Majeſty, and the Royal Race. Nor did he ever re-
pine either at his loſſes or ſufferings, but rejoyced rather
that he was able to ſuffer for His King and Countrey.
His Army was the onely Army that was able to up-
hold His Majeſties Power; which ſo long as it was
Victorious, it preſerved both His Majeſties Perſon and
Crown; but ſo ſoon as it fell, that fell too: and my
Lord was then in a manner forced to ſeek his own preſervation in foreign Countries, where God was pleaſed to make ſtrangers his Friends, who received and
protected him when he was baniſhed his native Country, and relieved him when his own Country-men
ſought to ſtarve him, by withholding from him what
was juſtly his own, onely for his Honeſty and Loy-

Y   alty;

alty; which relief he received more from the Commons of thofe parts where he lived, then from Princes, he being unwilling to trouble any foreign Prince with his wants and miferies, well knowing, that Gifts of Great Princes come flowly, and not without much difficulty; neither loves he to petition any one but His own Soveraign.

But though my Lord by the civility of Strangers, and the affiftance of fome few Friends of his native Country, lived in an indifferent Condition, yet (as it hath been declared heretofore) he was put to great plunges and difficulties, in fo much that his dear Brother Sir *Charles Cavendifh* would often fay, That though he could not truly complain of want, yet his meat never did him good, by reafon my Lord, his Brother, was always fo near wanting, that he was never fure after one meal to have another: And though I was not afraid of ftarving or begging, yet my chief fear was, that my Lord for his debts would fuffer Imprifonment, where fadnefs of Mind, and want of Exercife, and Air, would have wrought his deftruction, which yet by the Mercy of God he happily avoided.

Some time before the Reftauration of His Majefty to his Royal Throne, my Lord, partly with the remainder of his Brothers Eftate, which was but little, it being wafted by felling of Land for compounding with the Parliament, paying of feveral debts, and buying out the two Houfes aforementioned, *viz. Welbeck*

beck and *Bolsover* ; and the Credit which his Sons had
got, which amounted in all to 2400 l. a year, sprinkled
something amongst his Creditors, and borrowed so
much of Mr. *Top* and Mr. *Smith* (though without assu-
rance) that he could pay such scores as were most pres-
sing, contracted from the poorer sort of Trades-men,
and send ready mony to Market, to avoid cozenage (for
small scores run up most unreasonably, especially if
no strict accounts be kept, and the rate be left to the
Creditors pleasure) by which means there was in a
short time so much saved, as it could not have been ima-
gined.

About this time, a report came of a great number
of Sectaries, and of several disturbances in *England*,
which heightned my Lord's former hopes into a firm
belief of a sudden Change in that Kingdom, and a happy Restauration of His Majesty, which it also pleased
God to send according to his expectation ; for His
Majesty was invited by his Subjects, who were not a-
ble longer to endure those great confusions and encum-
brances they had sustained hitherto, to take possession
of His Hereditary Rights, aud the power of all his
Dominions: And being then at the *Hague* in *Holland*,
to take shipping in those parts for *England*, my Lord
went thither to wait on his Majesty, who used my
Lord very Graciously ; and his Highness the Duke
of *York* was pleased to offer him one of those Ships that
were ordered to transport His Majesty; for which he
returned,

returned his most humble thanks to his Highness,
and begg'd leave of His Highness that he might
hire a Vessel for himself and his Company.

In the mean time whilst my Lord was at the
Hague, His Majesty was pleased to tell him, That
General *Monk*, now Duke of *Albemarle*, had
desired the Place of being Master of the Horse:
To which my Lord answer'd, That that gallant Person was worthy of any Favour that His Majesty
could confer upon him: And having taken his leave
of His Majesty, and His Highness the Duke of *York*,
went towards the Ship that was to transport him
for *England*, (I might rather call it a Boat, then a
Ship; for those that were intrusted by my Lord to
hire a Ship for that purpose, had hired an old rot-
ten Fregat, that was lost the next Voyage after; insomuch, that when some of the Company that had
promised to go over with my Lord, saw it, they
turn'd back, and would not endanger their lives in
it, except the *now* Lord *Widdrington*, who was resolved not to forsake my Lord.)

My Lord (who was so transported with the joy
of returning into his Native Countrey, that he re-
garded not the Vessel) having set Sail from *Rotterdam*, was so becalmed, that he was six dayes and
six nights upon the Water, during which time he
pleased himself with mirth, and pass'd his time away
as well as he could; Provisions he wanted not, ha-
                                                    ving

ving them in great store and plenty.   At last being
come so far that he was able to discern the smoak of
London, which he had not seen in a long time, he
merrily was pleased to desire one that was near him,
to jogg and awake him out of his dream, for surely, said he, I have been sixteen years asleep, and am
not throughly awake yet. My Lord lay that night at
Greenwich, where his Supper seem'd more savoury
to him, then any meat he had hitherto tasted; and
the noise of some scraping Fidlers, he thought the
pleasantest harmony that ever he had heard.

In the mean time my Lords Son, *Henry* Lord
Mansfield, now Earl of *Ogle*, was gone to *Dover*
with intention to wait on His Majesty, and receive
my Lord, his Father, with all joy and duty, thinking he had been with His Majesty; but when he
miss'd of his design, he was very much troubled,
and more, when His Majesty was pleas'd to tell him,
That my Lord had set to Sea, before His Majesty
Himself was gone out of *Holland*, fearing my Lord
had met with some Misfortune in his Journey, because he had not heard of his Landing. Wherefore
he immediately parted from *Dover*, to seek my Lord,
whom at last he found at *Greenwich*; with what joy
they embraced and saluted each other, my Pen is too
weak to express.

But all this while, and after my Lord was gone
from *Antwerp*, I was left alone there with some of my
servants;

servants ; for my Lord being in *Holland* with His Majesty, declared in a Letter to me his intention of going for *England,* withal commanding me to stay in that City, as a Pawn for his debts, until he could compass money to discharge them ; and to excuse him to the Magistrates of the said City for not taking his leave of them, and paying his due thanks for their great civilities, which he desired me to do in his behalf. And certainly my Lords affection to me was such, that it made him very industrious in providing those means; for it being uncertain what or whether he should have any thing of his Estate, made it a difficult business for him to borrow Mony ; At last he received some of one Mr. *Ash,* now Sir *Joseph Ash,* a Merchant of *Antwerp,* which he returned to me ; but what with the expence I had made in the mean while, and what was required for my transporting into *England,* besides the debts formerly contracted, the said money fell too short by 400 l. and although I could have upon my own word taken up much more, yet I was unwilling to leave an engagement amongst strangers: Wherefore I sent for one Mr. *Shaw,* now Sir *John Shaw,* a near kindsman to the said Mr. *Ash,* intreating him to lend me 400 l. which he did most readily, and so discharged my debts.

My departure being now divulged in *Antwerp,* the Magistrates of the City came to take their leaves of me, where I desired one Mr. *Duart* a very worthy Gentleman,

man, and one of the chief of the City, though he de-
rives his Race from the *Portuguez* (to whom and his
Sisters, all very skilful in the Art of Musick, though
for their own pastime and Recreation, both my Lord
and my self were much bound for their great civilities) to be my Interpreter.   They were pleased to
express that they were sorry for our departure out of
their City, but withal rejoyced at our happy returning into our Native Country, and wished me soon
and well to the place where I most desired to be :
Whereupon I having excused my Lord's hasty going
away without taking his leave of them, returned them
mine and my Lord's hearty Thanks for their great civilities, declaring how sorry I was that it lay not in
my power to make an acknowledgment answerable to
them.   But after their departure from me, they were
pleased to send their Under-Officers (as the custom
there is) with a Present of Wine, which I received
with all respect and thankfulness.

I being thus prepar'd for my Voyage, went with
my Servants to *Flushing,* and finding no *English* Man of
War there, being loth to trust my self with a less Vessel, was at last informed that a *Dutch* man of War lay
there ready to Convoy some Merchants; I forthwith
sent for the Captain thereof, whose name was *Bankert,*
and asked him whether it was possible to obtain the favour of having the use of his Ship to transport me into
England? To which he answered, That he question'd

not

not but I might; for the Merchants which he was to convey, were not ready yet, defiring me to fend one of my fervants to the State, to requeft that favour of them; with whom he would go himfelf, and affift him the beft he could; which he alfo did. My fuit being granted, my felf and my chief fervants embarqued in the faid Ship; the reft, together with the Goods, being conveyed in another good ftrong Veffel, hired for that purpofe.

After I was fafely arrived at *London*, I found my Lord in Lodgings; I cannot call them unhandfome; but yet they were not fit for a Perfon of his Rank and Quality, nor of the capacity to contain all his Family: Neither did I find my Lord's Condition fuch as I expected: Wherefore out of fome paffion I defir'd him to leave the Town, and retire into the Countrey; but my Lord gently reproved me for my rafhnefs and impatience, and foon after removed into *Dorfet*-houfe; which, though it was better then the former, yet not altogether to my fatisfaction, we having but a part of the faid Houfe in poffeffion. By this removal I judged my Lord would not haftily depart from *London*; but not long after, he was pleafed to tell me, That he had difpatched his bufinefs, and was now refolved to remove into the Country, having already given order for Waggons to tranfport our goods, which was no unpleafant news to me, who had a great defire for a Countrey-life.

My

My Lord before he began his Journey, went to his Gracious Soveraign, and begg'd leave that he might retire into the Countrey, to reduce and settle, if possible, his confused, entangled, and almost ruined Estate. *Sir*, said he to His Majesty, *I am not ignorant, that many believe I am discontented; and 'tis probable they'l say, I retire through discontent: But I take God to witness, That I am in no kind or ways displeas'd; for I am so joyed at your Majesties happy Restauration, that I cannot be sad or troubled for any Concern to my own particular; but whatsoever Your Majesty is pleased to command me, were it to sacrifice my Life, I shall most obediently perform it; for I have no other Will, but Your Majesties Pleasure.*

Thus he kissed His Majesty's hand, and went the next day into *Nottingham-shire*, to his Mannor-house call'd *Welbeck*; but when he came there, and began to examine his Estate, and how it had been ordered in the time of his Banishment, he knew not whether he had left any thing of it for himself, or not, till by his prudence and wisdom he inform'd himself the best he could, examining those that had most knowledg therein. Some Lands, he found, could be recover'd no further then for his life, and some not at all: Some had been in the Rebels hands, which he could not recover, but by His Highness the Duke of *York*'s favour, to whom His Majesty had given all the Estates of those that were condemned and execu-

ted for murdering his Royal Father of blessed memory, which by the Law were forfeited to His Majesty; whereof His Highness graciously restor'd my
Lord so much of the Land that formerly had been
his, as amounted to 730 l. a year. And though my
Lord's Children had their Claims granted, and bought
out the Life of my Lord, their Father, which came
near upon the third part, yet my Lord received nothing for himself out of his own Estate, for the space
of eighteen years, viz. During the time from the first
entring into Warr, which was *June* 11. 1642, till
his return out of Banishment, *May* 28. 1660; for
though his Son *Henry*, now Earl of *Ogle*, and his
eldest Daughter, the now Lady *Cheiny*, did all what
lay in their power to relieve my Lord their Father,
and sent him some supplies of moneys at several
times when he was in banishment; yet that was of
their own, rather then out of my Lord's Estate; for
the Lady *Cheiny* sold some few Jewels which my Lord,
her Father, had left her, and some Chamber-Plate
which she had from her Grandmother, and sent o-
ver the money to my Lord, besides 1000 l. of her
Portion: And the now Earl of *Ogle* did at several
times supply my Lord, his Father, with such moneys as he had partly obtained upon Credit, and
partly made by his Marriage.

     After my Lord had begun to view those Ruines
that were nearest, and tried the Law to keep or recover

cover what formerly was his, (which certainly shew'd no favour to him, besides that the Act of Oblivion proved a great hinderance and obstruction to those his designs, as it did no less to all the Royal Party) and had setled so much of his Estate as possibly he could, he cast up the Summ of his Debts, and set out several parts of Land for the payment of them, or of some of them (for some of his Lands could not be easily sold, being entailed) and some he sold in *Derbyshire* to buy the Castle of *Nottingham*, which although it is quite ruined and demolisht, yet, it being a seat which had pleased his Father very much, he would not leave it since it was offer'd to be sold.

His two Houses *Welbeck* and *Bolsover* he found much out of repair, and this later half pull'd down, no furniture or any necessary Goods were left in them, but some few Hangings and Pictures, which had been saved by the care and industry of his Eldest Daughter the Lady *Cheiny*, and were bought over again after the death of his eldest Son *Charles*, Lord *Mansfield*; for they being given to him, and he leaving some debts to be paid after his death, My Lord sent to his other Son *Henry*, now Earl of *Ogle*, to endeavour for so much Credit, that the said Hangings and Pictures (which my Lord esteemed very much, the Pictures being drawn by *Van Dyke*) might be saved; which he also did, and My Lord hath paid the debt since his return.

Of

Of eight Parks, which my Lord had before the
Wars, there was but one left that was not quite deftroyed, *viz. Welbeck*-Park of about four miles compafs ; for my Lord's Brother Sir *Charles Cavendifh*,
who bought out the life of my Lord in that Lordfhip,
faved moft part of it from being cut down ; and in
Blore-Park there were fome few Deer left: The reft of the
Parks were totally defaced and deftroyed, both Wood,
Pales and Deer ; amongft which was alfo *Clipfton*-
Park of feven miles compafs, wherein my Lord had
taken much delight formerly, it being rich of Wood,
and containing the greateft and talleft Timber-trees of
all the Woods he had ; in fo much, that onely the
Pale-row was valued at 2000 l. It was water'd by a
pleafant River that runs through it, full of Fifh and
Otters ; was well ftock'd with Deer, full of Hares,
and had great ftore of Partriges, Poots, Pheafants, *&c*,
befides all forts of Water-fowl ; fo that this Park afforded all manner of fports, for Hunting, Hawking,
Courfing, Fifhing, *&c.* for which my Lord efteemed it very much: And although his Patience and Wifdom is fuch, that I never perceived him fad or difcon-
tented for his own Loffes and Misfortunes, yet when
he beheld the ruines of that Park, I obferved him
troubled, though he did little exprefs it, onely faying,
he had been in hopes it would not have been fo much
defaced as he found it, there being not one Timber-
tree in it left for fhelter.   However he patiently bore
what

what could not be helped, and gave present order for the cutting down of some Wood that was left him in a place near adjoining, to repale it, and got from several Friends Deer to stock it.

Thus though his Law-suits and other unavoidable expences were very chargeable to him, yet he order'd his affairs so prudently, that by degrees he stock'd and manur'd those Lands he keeps for his own use, and in part repaired his Mannor-houses, *Welbeck*, and *Bolsover*, to which later he made some additional building ; and though he has not yet built the Seat at *Nottingham*, yet he hath stock'd and paled a little Park belonging to it.

Nor is it possible for him to repair all the ruines of the Estate that is left him, in so short a time, they being so great, and his losses so considerable, that I cannot without grief and trouble remember them ; for before the Wars my Lord had as great an Estate as any subject in the Kingdom, descended upon him most by Women, *viz.* by his Grandmother of his Father's side, his own Mother, and his first Wife.

What Estate his Grandfather left to his Father Sir *Charles Cavendish*, I know not ; nor can I exactly tell what he had from his Grandmother, but she was very rich ; for her third Husband Sir *Will.* Saint *Loo*, gave her a good Estate in the West, which afterwards descended upon my Lord, my Lord's Mother being the younger daughter of the Lord *Ogle*, and sole

B b

Heir

Heir, after the death of her eldeſt Siſter *Jane*, Counteſs
of *Shrewsbury*, whom King *Charles* the Firſt reſtored
to her Fathers Dignity, *viz.* Baroneſs of *Ogle* : This
Title deſcended upon my Lord and his Heirs General,
together with 3000 l. a year in *Northumberland*; and
beſides the Eſtate left to my Lord, ſhe gave him
20000 l. in Money, and kept him and his Family at
her own charge for ſeveral years.

My Lord's firſt Wife, who was Daughter and Heir
to *William Baſſet* of *Blore* Eſq;, Widow to *Henry
Howard*, younger Son to *Thomas* Earl of *Suffolk*,
brought my Lord 2400 l. a Year Inheritance, between
ſix and ſeven thouſand Pounds in Money, and a join-
ture for her life of 800 l. a Year. Beſides my Lord
increaſed his own Eſtate before the Wars, to the value of 100000 l. and had increaſed it more, had not
the unhappy Wars prevented him; for though he had
ſome diſadvantages in his Eſtate, even before the
Wars, yet they are not conſiderable to thoſe he ſuffered afterwards for the ſervice of his King and Country : For example, His Father Sir *Charles Cavendiſh*
had lent his Brother in Law *Gilbert* Earl of *Shrewsbury* 16000 l. for which, although afterward before
his death he ſetled 2000 l. a year upon him; yet he
having injoyed the ſaid Money for many years without paying any uſe for it, it might have been improved
to my Lord's better advantage, had it been in his Fathers own hands, he being a Perſon of great prudence

in

in managing his Eftate; and though the faid Earl
of *Shrewsbury* made my Lord his Executor, yet my
Lord was fo far from making any advantage by
that Truft, even in what the Law allowed him, that
he loft 1700 l. by it; and afterwards delivered
up his Truft to *William* Earl of *Pembrook*, and *Thomas* Earl of *Arundel*, who both married two Daughters of the faid Earl of *Shrewsbury*; And fince his
return into *England*, upon the defire of *Henry Howard*, Second Son to the late Earl of *Arundel*, and
Heir apparent, (by reafon of his Eldeft Brother's
Diftemper) he refigned his Truft and Intereft to him,
which certainly is a very difficult bufinefs, and yet
queftionable whether it may lawfully be done, or
not? But fuch was my Lord's Love to the Family of the *Shrewsburies*, that he would rather wrong
himfelf, then it.

To mention fome lawful advantages which my
Lord might have made by the faid Truft, it may be
noted in the firft place, That the Earl of *Shrewsbury*'s
Eftate was Let in long Leafes, which, by the Law,
fell to the Executor. Next, that after fome Debts
and Legacies were paid out of thofe Lands, which
were fet out for that purpofe, they were fetled fo, that
they fell to my Lord. Thirdly, Seven hundred pounds
a year was left as a Gift to my Lord's Brother, Sir
Charles Cavendifh, in cafe the Countefs of *Kent*, Second Daughter to the faid Earl of *Shrewsbury*, had no
Chil-

Children.   But my Lord never made any advantage
for himself, of all these; neither was he inquifitive whether the faid Counteſs of *Kent* cut off the Entail of that
Land, although ſhe never had a Child ; for my Lord's
Nature is ſo generous, that he hates to be Mercenary,
and never minds his own Profit or Intereſt in any Truſt
or Employment, more then the good and benefit of
him that intruſts or employs him.

But, as I faid heretofore, theſe are but petty Loſſes in
compariſon of thoſe he ſuſtained by the late Civil
Warrs, whereof I ſhall partly give you an account: I
ſay partly; for though it may be computed what the
loſs of the Annual Rents of his Lands amounts to,
of which he never received the leaſt worth for himſelf
and his own profit, during the time both of his being
employed in the Service of Warr, and his *Sufferings* in
Baniſhment; as alſo the loſs of thoſe *Lands* that are alie-
nated from him, both in preſent poſſeſſion, and in
reverſion; and of his Parks and Woods that were cut
down; yet it is impoſſible to render an exact account
of his Perſonal Eſtate.

As for his Rents during the time he acted in the
Warrs, though he ſuffer'd others to gather theirs
for their own uſe, yet his own either went for the uſe
of the Army, or fell into the hands of the Enemy,
or were ſuppreſs'd and with-held from him by the
Cozenage of his Tenants and Officers, my Lord being then not able to look after them himſelf.

About

About the time when His late Majesty undertook the expedition into *Scotland* for the suppressing of some insurrection that happened there ; My Lord, as afore is mentioned , amongst the rest, lent His Majesty 10000 l. *sterling* ; But having newly married a Daughter to the then Lord *Brackly*, now Earl of *Bridgwater*, whose portion was 12000 l. the moiety whereof was paid in Gold on the day of her marriage, and the rest soon after (although she was too young to be bedded.) This, together with some other expences, caused him to take up the said 10000 l. at Interest, the Use whereof he paid many years after.

Also when after his sixteen years Banishment, he returned into *England*, before he knew what Estate was left him, and was able to receive any Rents of his own, he was necessitated to take 5000 l. upon Use for the maintenance of himself and his Family ; whereof the now Earl of *Devonshire*, his Cousin German, once removed, lent him 1000 l. for which and the former 1000 l. mentioned heretofore, he never desired nor received any Use from my Lord, which I mention, to declare the favour and bounty of that Noble Lord.

But though it is impossible to render an exact account of all the losses which My Lord has sustained by the said Wars, yet as far as they are accountable, I shall endeavour to represent them in these following Particulars :

C c   In

In the firſt place, I ſhall give you a juſt particular of My Lords Eſtate in Lands, as it was before the Wars, partly according to the value of his own Surveighers, and partly according to the rate it is let, at this preſent.

Next, I ſhall accompt the Woods cut down by the Rebellious Party, in ſeveral places of My Lords Eſtate.

Thirdly, I ſhall compute the Value of thoſe Lands which My Lord hath loſt, both in preſent poſſeſſion, and in reverſion; that is to ſay, thoſe which he has loſt altogether, both for himſelf, and his Poſterity ; and thoſe he has recovered onely during the time of his life, and which his onely Son and Heir, the now Earl of *Ogle,* muſt loſe after his Fathers deceaſe.

Fourthly, I ſhall make mention, how much of Land my Lord hath been forced to ſell for the payment of ſome of his Debts, contracted during the time of the late Civil Wars, and when his Eſtate was ſequeſtred ; I ſay ſome, for there are a great many to pay yet.

To which I ſhall, Fifthly, add the Compoſition of his Brothers Eſtate ; and the loſs of it for Eight years.

*A Particular of My Lords Estate in plain Rents,
as it was partly surveighed in the Year* 1641,
and partly is let at this present.

Nottingham-shire.

	l.	s.	d.		l.	s.	d.
The Mannor of *Welbeck*	0600	00	00				
The Mannor of *Norton, Carbarton,* and the *Granges*	0454	19	01				
Warksopp	0051	06	08				
The Mannor-house of *Soakholm*	0308	10	03				
The Manor of *Clipston* & *Edwinstow*	0334	09	08				
Drayton	0008	16	06		l.	s.	d.
Dunham	0099	17	08		6229	07	11
Sutton	0185	00	05				
The Mannor of *Kirby*, &c.	1075	07	02				
The Mannor of *Cotham*	0833	18	08				
The Mannor of *Sitthorp*	0704	01	00				
Carcholston	0450	03	00				
Hauksworth, &c.	0139	04	02				
Flawborough	0512	11	08				
Mearing and *Holm*-Meadow	0471	02	00				

Lincoln-shire.

	l.	s.	d.
Wellinger and *Ingham* Meales	0100	00	00

Derby-shire.

	l.	s.	d.		l.	s.	d.
The Barrony of *Bolsover* and *Woodthorp*	0846	08	11				
The Mannor of *Chesterfield*	0278	00	00				
The Mannor of *Barlow*	0796	17	06				
Tissington	0159	11	00				
Dronfield	0486	15	10				
The Mannor of *Brampton*	0142	04	08				
Little-*Longston*	0087	02	00				
The Mannor of *Stoak*	0212	03	00				
Birth-Hall, and *Peak*-Forrest	0131	08	00		6128	11	10
The Mannor of *Gringlow*	0156	08	00				
The Mannor of *Hucklow*	0162	10	08				
The Mannor of *Blackwall*	0306	00	04				
Buxton and *Tids-Hall*	0153	02	00				
Mansfield-Park	0100	00	00				
Mappleton and *Thorp*	0207	05	00				
The Mannor of *Windly*-Hill	0238	18	00				
The Mannor of *Litchurch* and *Markworth*	0713	15	01				
Church and *Meynel Langly* Mannor	0850	01	00				

Stafford-shire.

Stafford-shire.

	l.	s.	d.		l.	s.	d.
The Mannor of *Bloar* with *Caulton*	0573	13	04	⎫			
The Mannor of *Grindon, Cauldon*, with *Waterfull*	0822	03	00	⎬	2349	17	04
The Mannor of *Cheadle* with *Kinsly*	0259	18	00				
The Mannor of *Barleston*, &c.	0694	03	00	⎭			

Glocester-shire.

	l.	s.	d.		l.	s.	d.
The Manor of *Tormorton* with *Litleton*	1193	16	00	⎫	1581	19	02
The Mannor of *Acton Turvil*	0388	03	02	⎭			

Summerset-shire.

	l.	s.	d.		l.	s.	d.
The Mannor of *Chewstoak*	0816	15	06	⎫			
Knighton Sutton	0300	14	04	⎬	1303	13	10
Stroud and *Kingsham*-Park	0186	04	00	⎭			

York-shire.

		l.	s.	d.
The Manors of *Slingsby, Hoverngham* and *Friton, Northinges* and *Pomfret*		1700	00	00

Northumberland.

	l.	s.	d.
The Barrony of *Bothal, Ogle* and *Hepple*, &c.	3000	00	00

	l.	s.	d.
Totall	22393	10	01

That this Particular of My Lords Estate was no less then is mentioned, may partly appear by the rate, as it was surveighed, and sold by the Rebellious Parliament; for they raised, towards the later end of their power, which was in the year 1652, out of my Lords Estate, the summe of 111593 l. 10 s. 11 d. at five years and a half Purchase, which was at above the rate of 18000 l. a year, besides Woods; and his Brother

ther Sir *Charles Cavendish's* Eftate, which Eftate was
2000 l. a year, which falls not much fhort of the mentioned account ; and certainly, had they not fold fuch
Lands at eafie rates, few would have bought them, by
reafon the Purchafers were uncertain how long they
fhould enjoy their purchafe : Befides, Under-Officers
do not ufually refufe Bribes; and it is well known
that the Surveighers did under-rate Eftates according as
they were feed by the Purchafers.

Again, many of the Eftates of banifhed Perfons
were given to Soldiers for the payment of their Ar-
rears, who again fold them to others which would
buy them at eafier rates. But chiefly, it appears by
the rate as my Lords Eftate is let at prefent, there being feveral of the mentioned Lands that are let at a
higher rate now then they were furveighed ; nor are
they all valued in the mentioned particular according
to the furveigh, but many of them which were not
furveighed, are accounted according to the rate they are
let at at this prefent.

The Lofs of my Lords Eftate, in plain Rents, as
alfo upon ordinary Ufe, and Ufe upon Ufe, is as followeth:

The Annual Rent of My Lords Lands, *viz.*
22393 l. 10 s. 1 d. being loft for the fpace of 18
years, which was the time of his acting in the Wars,
and of his Banifhment, without any benefit to him,
reckoned without any Intereft, amounts to 40308 3 l.

D d   But

But being accounted with the ordinary Ufe at Six in the Hundred, and Ufe upon Ufe for the mentioned fpace of 18 Years, it amounts to 733579 l.

But fome perhaps will fay, That if My Lord had enjoyed his Eftate, he would have fpent it, at leaft fo much as to maintain himfelf according to his degree and quality.

I anfwer ; That it is very improbable My Lord fhould have fpent all his Eftate, if he had enjoyed it, he being a man of great Wifdom and Prudence, knowing well how to fpend, and how to manage ; for though he lived nobly before the time of the Wars, yet not beyond the Compafs of his Eftate ; nay, fo far he would have been from fpending his Eftate, that no doubt but he would have increaft it to a vaft value, as he did before the Wars; where notwithftanding his Hofpitality and noble Houfe-keeping, his charges of Building came to about 31000 l; the portion of his fecond Daughter, which was 12000 l; the noble entertainments he gave King *Charles* the Firft, one whereof came to almoft 15000 l. another to above 4000 l, and a third to 1700 l. as hereafter fhall be mentioned; and his great expences during the time of his being Governour to His Majefty that now is, he yet encreafed his Eftate to the value of 100000 l, which is 5000 *per annum*, when it was by fo much lefs.

But if any one will reckon the charges of his Houfekeeping during the time of his Exile, and when he
had

had not the enjoyment of his Estate, he may substract
the sum accounted for the payment of his debts, contracted in the time of his Banishment, which went to
the maintenance of himself and his Family ; or in
lieu thereof, considering that I do not account all My
Lords losses, but onely those that are certainly known,
he may compare it with the loss of his personal Estate,
whereof I shall make some mention anon, and he'll
find that I do not heighten my Lords Losses, but rather diminish them ; for surely the losses of his personal Estate, and those I account not, will counter-
ballance the charges of his House-keeping, if not ex-
ceed them.

Again, others will say, That there was much Land
sold in the time of My Lords Banishment by his Sons,
and Feoffees in Trust.

I answer, First, That whatsoever was sold, was first
bought of the Rebellious Power : Next, although
they sold some Lands, yet My Lord knew nothing of
it, neither did he receive a penny worth for himself, neither of what they purchased, nor sold, all the time of
his Banishment till his return.

And thus much of the loss of My Lords Estate in
Rents : Concerning the loss of his Parks and Woods,
as much as is generally known, (for I do not reckon
particular Trees cut down in several of his Woods yet
standing) 'tis as follows :

1. Clipston-

1. *Clipston-*Park and Woods cut down to the value of 20000 l.

2. *Kirkby-*Woods, for which my Lord was formerly proferr'd 10000 l.

3. Woods cut down in *Derbyshire* 8000 l.

4. *Red-lodg-*Wood, *Rome-*wood and others near *Welbeck* 4000 l.

5. Woods cut down in *Stafford-*shire 1000 l.

6. Woods cut down in *York-*shire 1000 l.

7. Woods cut down in *Northumberland* 1500 l.

The *Total* 45000 l.

The Lands which My Lord hath lost in present possession are 2015 l. *per annum*, which at 20 years purchase come to 40300 l. and those which he hath lost in Reversion, are 3214 l. *per annum*, which at 16 years, purchase amount to the value of 51424 l.

The Lands which my Lord since his return has sold for the payment of some of his debts, occasioned by the Wars (for I do not reckon those he sold to buy others) come to the value of 56000 l. to which out of his yearly revenue he has added 10000 l. more, which is in all 66000 l.

Lastly, The Composition of his Brothers Estate was 5000 l. and the loss of it for eight years comes to 16000 l.

All which, if summ'd up together, amounts to 941303 l.

These

These are the accountable losses, which My Dear
Lord and Husband has suffered by the late Civil
Wars, and his Loyalty to his King and Country.
Concerning the loss of his personal Estate, since (as
I often mentioned) it cannot be exactly known; I
shall not endeavour to set down the Particulars there-
of, onely in General give you a Note of what partly
they are:

1. The pulling down of several of his dwelling or
Mannor-houses.

2. The disfurnishing of them, of which the Furniture at *Bolsover* and *Welbeck* was very noble and rich:
Out of his *London*-house at *Clarken-well*, there were
taken, amongst other Goods, suits of Linnen, *viz.* Ta-
ble-Cloths, Sideboard-cloths, Napkins, &c. whereof one suit cost 160 l. they being bought for an Entertainment which My Lord made for Their Majesties,
King *Charles* the First, and the Queen, at *Bolsover*-
Castle; And of 150 Suits of Hangings of all sorts
in all his Houses, there were not above 10 or 12 saved.

Of Silver-plate, My Lord had so much as came to
the value of 3800 l. besides several Curiosities of Ca-
binets, Cups, and other things, which after My Lord
was gone out of *England*, were taken out of his Mannor-house, *Welbeck*, by a Garison of the Kings Party
that lay therein, whereof he recovered onely 1100 l.
which Money was sent him beyond the Seas, the rest
was lost.

E e   As

As for Pewter, Brass, Bedding, Linnen, and other Houshold-stuff, there was nothing else left but some few old Feather-beds, and those all spoiled, and fit for no use.

3. My Lord's Stock of Corn, Cattel, &c. was very great before the Warrs, by reason of the large-ness and capacity of those grounds, and the great number of Granges he kept for his own use; as for example, *Barlow*, *Carkholston*, *Gleadthorp*, *Welbeck*, and several more, which were all well manured and stockt. But all this stock was lost, besides his Race of Horses in his Grounds, Grange-Horses, Hackny-Horses, Mannage-Horses, Coach-Horses, and others he kept for his use.

To these Losses I may well and justly join the charges which my Lord hath been put to since his return into *England*, by reason they were caused by the ruines of the said Warrs; whereof I reckon,

1. His Law-suits, which have been very chargeable to him, more then advantagious.

2. The Stocking, Manuring, Paling, Stubbing, Hedging, &c. of his Grounds and Parks; where it is to be noted, That no advantage or benefit can be made of Grounds, under the space of three years, and of Cattel not under five or six.

3. The repairing and furnishing of some of his Dwelling-Houses.

4. The

4. The setting up a Race or Breed of Horses, as he had before the Warrs; for which purpose he hath bought the best Mares he could get for money.

In short, I can reckon 12000 l. laid out barely for the repair of some Ruines, which my Lord could not be without, there being many of them to repair yet; neither is this all that is laid out, but much more which I cannot well remember ; nor is there more but one Grange stock'd, amongst several that were kept for furnishing his House with Provisions :   As for other Charges and Losses, which My Lord hath sustained since his return , I will not reckon them, because my design is onely to account such losses as were caused by the Wars.

By which, as they have been mentioned, it may easily be concluded, That although My Lord's Estate was very great before the Wars, yet now it is shrunk into a very narrow compass, that it puts his Prudence and Wisdom to the Proof, to make it serve his necessities, he having no other assistance to bear him up; and yet notwithstanding all this, he hath since his return paid both for Himself and his Son, all manner of Taxes, Lones, Levies, Assessments, &c. equally with the rest of His Majesties Subjects, according to that Estate that is left him, which he has been forced to take upon Interest.

THE

The Third Book.

THus having given you a faithful Account of all My Lords Actions, both before, in, and after the Civil Warrs, and of his Losses; I shall now conclude with some particular heads concerning the description of his own Person, his Natural Humour, Disposition, Qualities, Vertues; his Pedigree, Habit, Diet, Exercises, &c. together with some other Remarks and Particulars which I thought requisite to be inserted, both to illustrate the former Books, and to render the History of his Life more perfect and compleat.

1. *Of his Power.*

After His Majesty King *Charles* the First, had entrusted my Lord with the Power of raising Forces for His Majesties Service, he effected that which never any Subject did, nor was (in all probability) able to do; for though many Great and Noble Persons did also raise Forces for His Majesty, yet they were Brigades, rather then well-formed Armies, in comparison to my Lord's. The reason was, That my Lord, by his Mother, the Daughter of *Cuthbert*

Lord

Lord *Ogle*, being allyed to moſt of the moſt ancient
Families in *Northumberland*, and other the Northern
parts, could pretend a greater Intereſt in them, then a
ſtranger; for they through a natural affection to my
Lord as their own Kinſman, would ſooner follow
him, and under his Conduct ſacrifice their Lives for
His Majeſty's Service, then any body elſe, well
knowing, That by deſerting my Lord, they deſert-
ed themſelves; and by this means my Lord raiſed
firſt a Troup of Horſe conſiſting of a hundred and
twenty, and a Regiment of Foot; and then an Army of Eight thouſand Horſe, Foot and Dragoons,
in thoſe parts; and afterwards upon this ground, at
ſeveral times, and in ſeveral places, ſo many ſeveral
Troups, Regiments and Armies, that in all from the
firſt to the laſt, they amounted to above 100000 men,
and thoſe moſt upon his own Intereſt, and without
any other conſiderable help or aſſiſtance; which was
much for a particular Subject, and in ſuch a conjuncture of time; for ſince Armies are ſooneſt raiſed by
Covetouſneſs, Fear aud Faction; that is to ſay, upon a conſtant and ſetled Pay, upon the Ground of
Terrour, and upon the Ground of Rebellion; but
very ſeldom or never upon uncertainty of Pay; and
when it is as hazardous to be of ſuch a Party, as to be
in the heat of a Battel; alſo when there is no other deſign but honeſt duty; it may eaſily be conceived that
my Lord could have no little love and affection when

F f   He

He raifed his Army upon fuch grounds as could promife them but little advantage at that time.

Amongft the reft of his Army, My Lord had chofen for his own Regiment of Foot, 3000 of fuch Valiant, ftout and faithful men, (whereof many were
bred in the Moorifh-grounds of the Northern parts)
that they were ready to die at my Lord's feet, and
never gave over, whenfoever they were engaged in
action, until they had either conquer'd the Enemy, or
loft their lives. They were called White-coats, for
this following reafon : My Lord being refolved to
give them new Liveries, and there being not red Cloth
enough to be had, took up fo much of white as would
ferve to cloath them, defiring withal, their patience until he had got it dyed; but they impatient of ftay, re-
quefted my Lord, that he would be pleafed to let them
have it un-dyed as it was, promifing they themfelves
would die it in the Enemies Blood : Which requeft my
Lord granted them, and from that time they were
called White-Coats.

To give you fome inftances of their Valour and
Courage, I muft beg leave to repeat fome paffages
mentioned in the firft Book. The Enemy having
clofely befieged the City of *York*, and made a paffage
into the Mannor-yard, by fpringing a Mine under
the Wall thereof, was got into the Mannor-houfe
with a great number of their Forces; which My Lord
perceiving, he immediately went and drew 80 of the
faid

said White-coats thither, who with the greatest Courage went close up to the Enemy, and having charged them, fell Pell-mell with the But-ends of their Musquets upon them, and with the assistance of the rest that renewed their Courage by their example, kill'd and took 1500, and by that means saved the Town.

How valiantly they behaved themselves in the last fatal Battel upon *Hessom-moor* near *York*, has been also declared heretofore; in so much, that although most of the Army were fled, yet they would not stir, until by the Enemies Power they were overcome, and most of them slain in rank and file.

Their love and affection to my Lord was such, that it lasted even when he was deprived of all his power, and could do them little good; to which purpose I shall mention this following passage:

My Lord being in *Antwerp*, received a Visit from a Gentleman, who came out of *England*, and rendred My Lord thanks for his safe Escape at Sea; My Lord being in amaze, not knowing what the Gentleman meant, he was pleased to acquaint Him, that in his coming over Sea out of *England*, he was set upon by Pickaroons, who having examined him, and the rest of his Company, at last some asked him, whether he knew the Marquess of *Newcastle*? To whom he answered, That he knew him very well, and was going over into the same City where my Lord lived. Whereupon they did not onely take nothing from

him,

him, but used him with all Civility, and desired him to remember their humble duty to their Lord General, for they were some of his White-Coats that had escaped death; and if my Lord had any service for them, they were ready to assist him upon what Designs soever, and to obey him in whatsoever he should be pleased to Command them.

This I mention for the Eternal Fame and Memory of those Valiant and Faithful Men. But to return to the *Power* my Lord had in the late Warrs: As he was the Head of his own Army, and had raised it most upon his own Interest for the Service of His Majesty; so he was never Ordered by His Majesty's Privy Council, (except that some Forces of His were kept by His late Majesty, (which he sent to Him) together with some Arms and Ammunition heretofore mentioned) until His Highness Prince *Rupert* came from His Majesty, to join with him at the Siege of *York*. He had moreover the Power of Coyning, Printing, Knighting, *&c.* which never any Subject had before, when His Soveraign Himself was in the Kingdom; as also the Command of so many Counties, as is mentioned in the First Book, and the Power of placing and displacing what Governours and Commanders he pleased, and of constituting what Garisons he thought fit; of the chief whereof I shall give you this following list.

A Par-

A Particular of the Principal Garisons, and the Go-
vernors of them, constituted by my Lord.

In Northumberland.

NEwcastle upon *Tyne*, Sir *John Marley* Knight.
Tynmouth-Castle and *Sheilds*, Sir *Thomas Riddal*,
Knight.

In the Bishoprick of Durham.

Hartlepool, Lieutenant Colonel *Henry Lambton*.
Raby-Castle, Sir *William Savile*, Knight and Baronet.

In Yorkshire.

The City of *York*, Sir *Thomas Glenham* Knight and
Baronet; and afterwards when he took the Field,
the Lord *Jo. Bellasyse*.
Pomfret-Castle, Colonel *Mynn*, and after him Sir *Jo.*
Redman.
Sheffield-Castle, Major *Beamont*.
Wortly-Hall, Sir *Francis Wortley*.
Tickhill-Castle, Major *Mountney*.
Doncaster, Sir *Francis Fane*, Knight of the Bath, af-
terwards Governour of *Lincoln*.
Sandal-Castle, Captain *Bonivant*.

Gg   *Skipton*

Skipton-Caftle, Sir *John Mallary*, Baronet.

Bolton-Caftle, Mr. *Scroope*.

Hemfley-Caftle, Sir *Jordan Crofland*.

Scarborough-Caftle and Town, Sir *Hugh Chomley*.

Stamford-Bridg, Colonel *Galbreth*.

Hallifax, Sir *Francis Mackworth*.

Tadcafter, Sir *Gamaliel Dudley*.

Eyrmouth, Major *Kaughton*.

In Cumberland.

The City of *Carlifle*, Sir *Philip Mufgrave*, Knight
    and Baronet.

Cockermouth, Colonel *Kirby*.

In Nottinghamfhire.

Newark upon *Trent*, Sir *John Henderfon*, Knight; and
    afterwards, Sir *Richard Byron*, Knight, now Lord
    Byron.

Wyrton-Houfe, Colonel *Rowland Hacker*.

Welbeck, Colonel *Van Peire*; and after, Colonel
    Beeton.

Shelford-Houfe, Col. *Philip Stanhop*.

In Lincolnſhire.

The City of *Lincoln*, firſt Sir *Francis Fane*, Knight of the Bath ; ſecondly, Sir *Peregrine Bartu.*
Gainsborough,   Colonel St. *George.*
Bullingbrook-Caſtle,   Lieutenant Colonel *Cheſter.*
Beluoir-Caſtle,   Sir *Gervas Lucas.*

In Derbyſhire.

Bolſover-Caſtle,   Colonel *Muſchamp.*
Wingfield Mannor,   Colonel *Roger Molyneux.*
Staly-Houſe, the now Lord *Fretchwile.*

A L I S T *of the General* O F F I C E R S *of the* A R M Y.

1. THe Lord General, the now Duke of *Newca-ſtle*, the Noble Subject of this Book.

2. The Lieutenant General of the Army ; firſt the Earl of *Newport*, afterwards the Lord *Eythin.*

3. The General of the Ordnance, *Charles* Viſcount *Mansfield.*

4. The General of the Horſe, *George* Lord *Goring.*

5. The

5. The Colonel General of the Army, Sir *Thomas Glenham.*

6. The Major General of the Army, Sir *Francis Mackworth.*

7. The Lieutenant General of the Horse, First Mr. *Charles Cavendish*, after him Sir *Charles Lucas.*

8. Commiſſary General of Horse, First Colonel *Windham*, after him Sir *William Throckmorton*, and after him Mr. *George Porter.*

9. Lieutenant General of the Ordnance, Sir *William Davenant.*

10. Treaſurer of the Army, Sir *William Carnaby.*

11. Advocate-General of the Army, Dr. *Liddal.*

12. Quarter-Maſter General of the Army, Mr. *Ralph Errington.*

13. Providore-General of the Army, Mr. *Gervas Nevil*, and after Mr. *Smith.*

14. Scout-Maſter-General of the Army, Mr. *Hudſon.*

15. Waggon-Maſter-General of the Army, *Baptiſt Johnſon.*

William

William Lord *Widdrington* was Prefident of the Council of War, and Commander in chief of the three Counties of *Lincoln,* *Rutland* and *Nottingham,* and the forces there.

When my Lord marched with his Army to *New-caftle* againſt the *Scots,* then the Lord *John Bellaſſis* was conſtituted Governour of *York,* and Commander in Chief, or Lieutenant General of *York-ſhire.*

As for the reſt of the Officers and Commanders of every particular Regiment and Company, they being too numerous, cannot well be remembred, and therefore I ſhall give you no particular accompt of them.

2. *Of His Misfortunes and obſtruƈtions.*

ALthough Nature had favour'd My Lord, and endued him with the beſt Qualities and Perfeƈtions ſhe could inſpire into his ſoul ; yet Fortune hath ever been ſuch an inveterate Enemy to him, that ſhe invented all the ſpight and malice againſt him that lay in her power; and notwithſtanding his prudent Counſels and Deſigns, caſt ſuch obſtruƈtions in his way, that he ſeldom proved ſucceſsful, but where he aƈted in Perſon. And ſince I am not ignorant that this unjuſt and

partial

partial Age is apt to suppress the worth of meritorious
persons, and that many will endeavour to obscure my
Lords noble Actions and Fame, by casting unjust a-
spersions upon him, and laying (either out of igno-
rance or malice) Fortunes envy to his charge, I have
purposed to represent these obstructions which conspi-
red to render his good intentions and endeavours ineffectual, and at last did work his ruine and destruction,
in these following particulars.

1. At the time when the Kingdom became so in-
fatuated, as to oppose and pull down their Gracious
King and Soveraign, the Treasury was exhausted,
and no sufficient means to raise and maintain Armies to
reduce his Majesties Rebellious Subjects; so that My
Lord had little to begin withal but what his own Estate
would allow, and his Interest procure him.

2. When his late Majesty, in the beginning of the
unhappy Wars, sent My Lord to *Hull*, the strongest
place in the Kingdom, where the Magazine of Arms
and Ammunition was kept, and he by his prudence
had gained it to his Majesties service; My Lord
was left to the mercy of the Parliament, where he
had surely suffered for it, (though he acted not without His Majesties Commission) if some of the contrary party had not quitted him, in hopes to gain him
on their side.

3. After

3. After His Majesty had sent My Lord to *Newcastle* upon *Tyne*, to take upon him the Government of that place, and he had raised there, of Friends and Tenants, a troup of Horse and Regiment of Foot, which he ordered to conveigh some Arms and Ammunition to His Majesty, sent by the Queen out of *Holland*; His Majesty was pleased to keep the same Convoy with him to encrease his own Forces, which although it was but of a small number, yet at that present time it would have been very serviceable to my Lord, he having then but begun to raise Forces.

4. When Her Majesty the now Queen-Mother, after her arrival out of *Holland* to *York*, had a purpose to conveigh some Armes to His Majesty, My Lord order'd a Party of 1500 to conduct the same, which His Majesty was pleased to keep with him for his own service.

5. After Her Majesty had taken a resolution to go from *York* to *Oxford*, where the King then was; my Lord for Her safer conduct quitted 7000 men of his Army, with a convenient Train of Artillery, which likewise never returned to my Lord.

6. When the Earl of *Montross* was going into *Scotland*, he went to my Lord at *Durham*, and desired of him a supply of some Forces for His Majesties service; where my Lord gave him 200 Horse and Dragoons, even at such a time when he stood most in need of a supply himself, and thought every day to encounter the *Scottish* Army.

H h

7. When

7. When my Lord out of the Northern parts went into *Lincoln-* and *Derby-shires* with his Army, to order and reduce them to their Allegiance and Duty to His Majesty, and from thence resolved to march into the Associate Counties, (where in all porbability he would have made an happy end of the Warr) he was so importuned by those he left behind him, and particularly the Commander in Chief, to return into *York-shire*, alledging the Enemy grew strong, and would ruine them all, if he came not speedily to succour and assist them; that in honour and duty he could do no otherwise but grant their Requests; when as yet being returned into those parts he found them secure and safe enough from the Enemies Attempts.

8. My Lord (as heretofore mentioned) had as great private Enemies about His Majesty, as he had publick Enemies in the Field, who used all the endeavour they could to pull him down.

9. There was such Jugling, Treachery, and Falshood in his own Army, and amongst some of his own Officers, that it was impossible for my Lord to be prosperous and successful in his Designs and Undertakings.

10. My Lord's Army being the chief and greatest Army which His Majesty had, and in which consisted His prime Strength and Power; the Parliament resolved at last, to join all their Forces with the Army

of

of the *Scots*, (which when it came out of *Scotland*, was above Twenty thousand Men) to oppose, and if possible, to ruine it; well knowing, that if they did pull down my Lord, they should be Masters of all the Three Kingdoms; so that there were Three Armies against One.   But although my Lord suffered much by the Negligence (and sometimes Treachery) of his Officers, and was unfortunately called back into *York-shire*, from his March he designed for the Associate Counties, and was forced to part with a great number of his Forces and Ammunition, as aforementioned; yet he would hardly have been overcome, and his Army ruined by the Enemy, had he but had some timely supply and assistance at the Siege of *York*, or that his Counsel had been taken in not fighting the Enemy then, or that the Battel had been differ'd some two or three dayes longer, until those Forces were arrived which he expected, namely three thousand men out of *Northumberland*, and Two thousand drawn out of several Garisons.   But the chief Misfortune was, That the Enemy fell upon the Kings Forces before they were all put into a *Battallia*, and took them at their great disadvantage; which caused such a Panick fear amongst them, that most of the Horse of the right Wing of His Majesty's Forces, betook themselves to their heels; insomuch, that although the left Wing (commanded by the Lord *Goring*, and my Brother Sir *Charles Lucas*) did their best endeavour, and

beat

beat back the Enemy three times, and My Lord's own Regiment of Foot charged them so couragiously, that they never broke, but died most of them in their Ranks and Files ; yet the Power of the Enemy being too strong, put them at last to a total rout and confusion. Which unlucky disaster put an end to all future hopes of His Majesties Party ; so that my Lord seeing he had nothing left in his Power to do His Majesty any further service in that kind (for had he stayed, he would have been forced to surrender all those Towns and Garisons in those parts, that were yet in His Majesties Devotion, as afterwards it also happen'd) resolved to quit the Kingdom, as formerly is mentioned.

And these are chiefly the obstructions to the good success of my Lord's Designs in the late Civil Wars ; which being rightly considered, will save him blameless from what otherwise would be laid to his charge ; for, as according to the old saying, *'Tis easie for men to swim, when they are held up by the chin* : So on the other side, it is very dangerous and difficult for them to endeavour it, when they are pulled down by the Heels, and beaten upon their Heads.

3. *Of His Loyalty and Sufferings.*

I dare boldly and justly say, That there never was, nor is a more Loyal and Faithful Subject then My
Lord :

Lord: Not to mention the Truft he difcharged in all thofe imployments, which either King *James*, or King *Charles* the Firft, or His now Gracious Mafter King *Charles* the Second, were pleafed to beftow upon him, which he performed with fuch care and fidelity, that he never difobeyed their Commands in the leaft; I will onely note,

1. That he was the Firft that appear'd in Armes for His Majefty, and engaged Himfelf and all his Friends he could for His Majefties Service; and though he had but two Sons which were young, and one onely Brother, yet they all were with him in the Wars: His two Sons had Commands, but His Brother, though he had no Command, by reafon of the weaknefs of his body, yet he was never from My Lord when he was in action, even to the laft; for he was the laft with my Lord in the Field in that fatal Battel upon *Heffom-moor*, near *York*; and though my Brother, Sir *Charles Lucas*, defired my Lord to fend his Sons away, when the faid Battel was fought, yet he would not, faying, His Sons fhould fhew their Loyalty and Duty to His Majefty, in venturing their lives, as well as Himfelf.

2. My Lord was the chief and onely Perfon, that kept up the Power of His late Majefty; for when his Army was loft, all the Kings Party was ruined in all three of his Majefties Kingdoms; becaufe in his Army lay the chief ftrength of all the Royal Forces;

I i

it

it being the greateſt and beſt formed Army which His
Majeſty had, and the onely ſupport both of his Ma-
jeſties Perſon and Power, and of the hopes of all his
Loyal Subjects in all his Dominions.

3. My Lord was 16 Years in Baniſhment, and
hath loſt and ſuffered moſt of any ſubject, that ſuffer'd
either by War, or otherways, except thoſe that loſt
their lives, and even that he valued not, but exp'ſd
it to ſo eminent dangers that nothing but Heavens De-
cree had ordained to ſave it.

4. He never minded his own Intereſt more then
his Loyaltie and Duty, and upon that account never
deſired nor received any thing from the Crown to enrich himſelf, but ſpent great ſums in His Majeſties Service; ſo that after his long baniſhment and return into
England, I obſerved his ruined Eſtate was like an
Earthquake, and his Debts like Thunder-bolts, by
which he was in danger of being utterly undone, had
not Patience and Prudence, together with Heavens
Bleſſings, ſaved him from that threatning Ruine.

5. He never repined at his Loſſes and Sufferings, becauſe he loſt and ſuffered for his King and Countrey;
nay, ſo far was he from that, that I have heard him
ſay, If the ſame Warrs ſhould happen again, and he
was ſure to loſe both his life, and all he had left him, yet
he would moſt willingly ſacrifice it for His Majeſties
Service.

6. He

6. He never connived or confpired with the Enemy, neither directly nor indirectly; for though fome
Perfon of Quality being fent in the late Wars to him
into the North, from His late Majefty, who was
then at *Oxford*, with fome Meffage, did withal in private acquaint him, that fome of the Nobility that were
with the King, defired him to fide with them againft
His Majefty, alledging that if His Majefty fhould become an abfolute Conqueror, both himfelf and the reft
of the Nobility would lofe all their Rights and Priviledges; yet he was fo far from confenting to it, that
he returned him this anfwer, namely, That he entred
into actions of War, for no other end, but for the
fervice of His King and Mafter, and to keep up His
Majefties Rights and Prerogatives, for which he was
refolved to venture both his Life, Pofterity and Eftate;
for certainly, faid he, the Nobility cannot fall if the
King be Victorious, nor can they keep up their Dignities, if the King be overcome.

This Meffage was delivered by word of mouth, but
none of their names mentioned; fo that it is not certainly known whether it was a real truth or not; more
probable it was, that they intended to found my Lord,
or to make, if poffible, more divifion; for certainly
not all that pretended to be for the King, were His
Friends; and I my felf remember very well, when I
was with Her Hajefty, the now Queen-Mother, in
Oxford, (although I was too young to perceive their
intrigues,

intrigues, yet I was old enough to obferve) that there were great Factions both amongft the Courtiers and Soldiers. But my Lords Loyalty was fuch, that he kept always faithful and true to His Majefty, and could by no means be brought to fide with the Rebellious Party, or to juggle and mind his own Intereft more then his Majefties Service; and this was the caufe that he had as great private Enemies at Court, as he had publick Enemies in the Field, who fought as much his ruine and deftruction privately, and would caft afperfions upon his Loyalty and Duty, as thefe did publickly oppofe him.

In fhort, that it may appear the better what loyal and faithful fervices my Lord has done both for His late Majefty King *Charles* the Firft, and His now Gracious Mafter King *Charles* the Second, I have thought fit to fubjoin both Their Majefties Commendations which they were pleafed to give him, when for his Great and Loyal Services they confer'd upon him the Titles and Dignities of *Marquefs*, and *Duke of Newcaftle*.

A

A Copy of the Preamble of My Lord's Patent for *Marqueſs*, Engliſhed.

Rex *&c.* Salutem.

WHereas *it appears to Us, That* William *Earl* of Newcaſtle *upon* Tyne *, beſides his moſt Eminent Birth and ſplendid Alliances , hath equalled all thoſe Titles with which he is adorned by Deſert, and hath alſo wonne them by Virtue, Induſtry, Prudence, and a ſtedfaſt Faith : Whileſt with dangers and expences gathering together Soldiers, Armes, and all other War-like Habiliments ; and applying them as well in Our Affairs, as moſt plentifully ſending them to Us, (having fore-thought of Our Dignity and ſecurity) he was ready with Us in all Actions in* York-ſhire, *and governed the Town of* Newcaſtle, *and Caſtle in the mouth of* Tyne, *at the time of that fatal Revolt of the People who were got together; and with a Bond of his Friends did opportunely ſeize that Port, and ſettled it a Gariſon; bringing Armes to Us (then Our onely relief:) In which Service ſo ſtrongly going on, (which was of grand moment to our affairs) We do gratefully remember him ſtill to have ſtood to : Afterwards, having Muſtered together a good Army, (Our ſelf being gone elſe-where) the Rebels now enjoying almoſt all* York-ſhire, *and the chiefeſt Fortreſs of all the Country now appearing to have ſcarce refuge or ſafety for him againſt the ſwelling Rebels, (the*

K k   *whole*

*whole Country then desiring and praying for his coming,
that he might timely relieve them in their desperate condition) And leading his said Army in the midst of Winter,
gave the Rebels Battel in his passage, vanquish'd them, and
put them to flight, and took from them several Garisons,
and places of Refuge, and restored Health to the Subjects,
and by his many Victories,* Peace and Security *to the Coun-
tryes: Witness those places, made Noble by the death and
flight of the Rebels: in Lincoln-shire,* Gainsborough
and Lincoln; *in Derby-shire,* Chesterfield; *but in*
York-shire, Peirce-bridge, Seacroft, Tankerly, Tadcaster, Sheffield, Rotheram, Yarum, Beverly, Cawood, Selby, Halifax, Leeds, *and above all,* Bradford; *where when the* Yorkshire-*and* Lancashire-*Rebels
were united, and Battel joined with them; when Our Army as well by the great numbers of the Rebels, as much more
the badness of Our ground, was so prest upon, that the Soldiers now seemed to think of flying; He, their General, with
a full Carier, commanding two Troops to follow him,
broke into the very rage of the Battel, and with so much vi-
olence fell upon the right Wing of those Rebels, That those
who were but now certain of Victory, turn'd their backs, and
fled from the Conqueror, who by his Wisdom, Virtue and
his own Hand, brought death and flight to the Rebels, Victory and Glory to Himself, Plunder to the Soldiery,
and* 22 *great Guns, and many Ensigns to Us. Nor was
there before this, wanting to so much Virtue, equal Felicity,
for Our most beloved Consort, after a dismal Tempest coming*
                                  from

from Holland, *being drove afhore at* Burlington, *and undergoing a more grievous danger, by the excurfions of the Rebels, then the toffing and tumbling of the Sea; He having heard of it, fpeedily goes to Her with his Army, and dutifully receiveth Her, in fafety brings Her, and with all fecurity conducts Her to* Us *at* Oxford. *Whereas therefore the aforefaid Earl hath raifed fo many Monuments of His Virtue and Fidelity towards* Us, *Our Queen, Children, and Our Kingdom; when alfo he doth at this time eftablifh with fafety, and with His Power defend the Nothern parts of Our Kingdom againft the Rebels; when laftly, nothing more concerns Mankind and Princes, and nothing can be more juft, then that he may receive for his Deeds, a Reward fuitable to his name, which requires that he who defends the Borders, fhould be created by* Us, Governour *or* Marquefs of the Borderers. *Know therefore, &c.*

A

A Copy of the Preamble of My Lord's Patent for *DUKE*, Englished.

Rex &c. Salutem.

*W*Hereas Our *most beloved and faithful Cousin and Counsellor*, William *Earl and Marquess of* Newcastle upon Tyne, &c. *worthy by his famous Name, Blood and Office, of large Honours, has been eminent in so many, and so great Services performed to Us and Our Father (of ever blessed memory) that his Merits are still producing new effects, We have decreed likewise to add more Honour to his former. And though these his such eminent Actions, which he hath faithfully and valiantly performed to Us, Our Father, and Our Kingdom, speak loud enough in themselves; yet since the valiant Services of a good Subject are always pleasant to remember, We have thought fit to have them in part related for a good Example and Encouragement to Virtue.*

The great proofs of his Wisdom and Piety are sufficiently known to Us from Our younger years, and We shall alwayes retain a sense of those good Principles he instilled into Us; the Care of Our Youth which he happily undertook for Our good, he as faithfully and well discharged. Our years growing up amidst bad Times, and the harsh Necessities of Warr, a new Charge and Care of Loyaltie, the Kingdom

and

and Religion call'd him off to make use of his further Diligence and Valour. Rebellion spread abroad, he levied Loyal Forces in great numbers, opposed the Enemy; won so many and so great Victories in the Field, took in so many Towns, Castles and Garisons, as well in Our Northern parts, as elsewhere; and behaved himself with so great Courage and Valour in the defending also what he had got, especially at the Siege of York, *which he maintain'd against three Potent Armies of Scots and English, closely beleaguering, and with emulation assaulting it for three Months (till Relief was brought) to the wonder and envy of the Enemy; that, if Loyal and Humane Force could have prevailed, he had soon restored Fidelity, Peace and his* KING *to the Nation; which was then hurrying to Ruine by an unhappy Fate; So that Rebellion getting the upper hand, and no place being left for him to act further valiantly in, for his King and Countrey, he still retain'd the same Loyalty and Valour in suffering, being an inseparable Follower of Our Exile; during which sad Catastrophe, his whole Estate was sequestred and sold from him, and his Person alwayes one of the first of those few who were excepted both for Life and Estate (which was offer'd to all others.) Besides, his Virtues are accompanied with a Noble Blood, being of a Family by each Stock equally adorn'd and endow'd with great Honours and Riches. For which Reasons We have resolv'd to grace the said Marquess with a new Mark of our Favour, he being every way deserv-*

L l

ing

*ing of it, as one who lov'd vertue equal to his Noble
Birth, and possess'd Patrimonies suitable to both, as long as
loyalty had any place to shew it self in our Realm; which
possessions he so well employ'd, and at last for Us and Our
Fathers service lost, till he was with Us restor'd. Know
therefore, &c.*

4. Of his Prudence and Wisdom.

MY Lord's Prudence and Wisdom hath been sufficiently apparent both in his Publick and Private Actions and Imployments; for he hath such a
Natural Inspection, and Judicious Observation of
things, that he sees beforehand what will come to pass,
and orders his affairs accordingly. To which purpose I cannot but mention, that *Laud*, the then Arch-
bishop of *Canterbury*, between whom and my Lord,
interceded a great and intire Friendship, which he con-
firmed by a Legacy of a Diamond, to the value of
200 l. left to my Lord when he died, which was much
for him to bequeath; for though he was a great States-
man, and in favour with his late Majesty, yet he was
not covetous to hoard up wealth, but bestowed it rather upon the Publick, repairing the Cathedral of
St. *Pauls* in *London*, which, had God granted him life,
he would certainly have beautified, and rendred as
famous and glorious as any in Christendom: This said
                                              Arch-Bishop

Arch-Bifhop was pleafed to tell His late Majefty, that my Lord was one of the Wifeft and Prudenteft Perfons that ever he was acquainted with.

For further proof, I cannot pafs by that my Lord told His late Majefty King *Charles* the Firft, and Her Majefty the now Queen-Mother, fome time before the Wars, That he obferved by the humours of the People, the approaching of a Civil War, and that His Majefties Perfon would be in danger of being depofed, if timely care was not taken to prevent it.

Alfo when my Lord was at *Antwerp*, the Marquefs of *Montrofs*, before he went into *Scotland*, gave my Lord a Vifit, and acquainted him with his intended Journey, asking my Lord whether he was not alfo going for *England*? My Lord anfwer'd, He was ready to do His Majefty what fervice he could, and would fhun no opportunity, where he perceived he could effect fomething to His Majefties advantage; Nay, faid he, if His Majefty fhould be pleafed to Command my fingle Perfon to go againft the whole Army of the Enemy, although I was fure to lofe my life, yet out of a Loyal Duty to His Majefty, and in Obedience to his Commands, I fhould never refufe it. But to venture (faid he) the life of my Friends, and to betray them in a defperate action, without any probability of doing the leaft good to His Majefty, would be a very unjuft and unconfcionable act ; for my Friends might perhaps venture with me upon an implicite

plicite Faith, that I was so honest as not to engage
them without a firm and solid foundation ; but I
wanting that, as having no Ships, Armes, Ammunition, Provision, Forts, and places of Rendezvous, and what is the chief thing, Money; To what
purpose would it be to draw them into so hazardous an
Action, but to seek their ruine and destruction, without the least benefit to His Majesty ? Then the Marquess
of *Montross* asked my Lord's Advice, and what he
should do in such a case? My Lord answer'd, That
he knowing best his own Countrey, Power and
Strength, and what probability he had of Forces,
and other Necessaries for Warr, when he came into
Scotland, could give himself the best advice; but
withall told him, That if he had no Provision nor
Ammunition, Armes and places of Rendezvous
for his men to meet and join, he would likely be
forced to hide his head, and suffer for his rash undertaking: Which unlucky Fate did also accordingly befall that worthy Person.

Thesé passages I mention to no other end, but to
declare my Lord's Judgment and Prudence in world-
ly Affairs; whereof there are so many, that if I
should set them all down, it would swell this History to a big Volume. They may in some sort be gather'd
from his actions mentioned heretofore, especially the
ordering of his affairs in the time of Warr, with
such Conduct, Prudence and Wisdom, that not-
with-

withstanding at the beginning of his Undertaking that
great Trust and honourable Employment which His
late Majesty was pleased to confer upon him, he saw
so little appearance of performing his Designs with
good success, His Majesty's Revenues being then much
weakned, and the Magazines and publick Purse, in the
Enemies Power, besides several other obstructions
and hinderances; yet as he undertook it chearfully,
and out of pure Loyalty and Obedience to His Majesty; so he ordered it so wisely, that so long as he a-
cted by his own Counsels, and was personally present
at the execution of his Designs, he was always prosperous in his Success. And although he had so great
an Army, as aforementioned, yet by his wise and
prudent Conduct, there appear'd no visible sign of de-
vastation in any of the Countreys where he marched;
for first, he setled a constant Rule for the Regular levy of money for the convenient Maintenance of the
Soldiery. Next, he constituted such Officers of his
Army, that most of them were known to be Gentlemen of large and fair Estates, which drew a good part
of their private Revenues, to serve and support them
in their publick Employments; wherein my Lord did
lead them the way by his own good Example.

To which may be added his wisdom in ordering the
Government of the Church, for the advancement of the
Orthodox Religion, and suppression of Factions; as
also in Coyning, Printing, Knighting, and the like,

M m   which

which he used with great difcretion and prudence, one-ly for the Intereft of His Majefty, and the benefit of the Kingdom , as formerly has been mentioned.

The Prudent mannage of his private and dome-ftick affairs, appears fufficiently : 1. In his Marriage. 2. In the ordering and increafing his Eftate before the Wars , which notwithftanding his Noble Houfe-keeping and Hofpitality, and his Generous Bounty and Charity, he increafed to the value of 100000 l. 3. In the ordering his Affairs in the time of Banifh-ment, where although he received not the leaft of his own eftate, during all the time of his exile, until his return; yet maintained himfelf handfomely and no-bly, according to his Quality, as much as his Condi-tion at that time would permit. 4. In reducing his torn and ruined Eftate after his return, which beyond all probability, himfelf hath fetled and order'd fo, that his Pofterity will have reafon gratefully to remember it.

In fhort ; Although my Lord naturally loves not bufinefs, efpecially thofe of State, (though he under-ftands them as well as any body) yet what bufinefs or affairs he cannot avoid, none will do them better then himfelf. His private affairs he orders without a-ny noife or trouble, not over-haftily, but wifely : Nei-ther is he paffionate in acting of bufinefs, but hears pa-tiently, and orders foberly, and pierces into the heart or bottom of a bufinefs at the firft encounter ; but be-fore all things, he confiders well before he undertakes a bufinefs, whether he be able to go through it or no, for he never ventures upon either publick or private bufinefs, beyond his ftrength.

And here I cannot forbear to mention, that my Noble Lord, when he was in banifhment, prefumed out of his Duty and Love to his Gracious Mafter our now Soveraign King *Charles* the Second, to write and fend him a little Book, or rather a Letter, wherein he delivered his Opinion concerning the Government of his Dominions, whenfoever God fhould be pleafed to reftore him to his Throne, together with fome other Notes and Obfervations of Foreign States and Kingdoms; but it being a private offer to His facred Majefty, I dare not prefume to publifh it.

5. *Of His Bleffings.*

ALthough my Lord hath been one of the moft Unfortunate Perfons of his Rank and Quality, which this later age did produce; yet Heaven hath been fo propitious to him, that it beftowed fome bleffings upon him even in the midft of his Misfortunes, and fupported him againft Fortunes Malice, which otherwife, as it feems, had defigned his total ruine and deftruction: Of thefe Bleffings I may name in the firft place,

1. The Royal Favours of His Gracious Soveraign's

raign's, and the good esteem they had of his Fidelity and Loyalty; which as it was the chief of his endeavours, so he esteemed it above all the rest. To repeat them particularly would be too tedious, and they are sufficiently apparent out of the precedent History; onely this I may add, that King *Charles* the First, out of a singular Favour to my Lord, was pleased upon his most humble request, to create several Noble-men; the Names of them, lest I commit an offence, I shall not mention, by reason most men usually pretend such claimes upon the Ground of their own Merit.

2. That God was pleased to bless him with Wealth and Power, to enable him the better for the service of his King and Country.

3. That he made him happy in his Marriage ; (for his first Wife was a very kind, loving and Virtuous Lady) and bless'd him with Dutiful and Obedient Children, free from Vices , Noble and Generous both in ther Natures and Actions ; who did all that lay in their power to support and relieve my Lord their Father in his Banishment, as before is mentioned.

4. The Kindness and Civility which my Lord received from Strangers, and the Inhabitants of those places, where he lived during the time of his Banishment ; for had it not been for them, he would have perished in his extream wants ; but it pleased God so to provide for him, that although he wanted an Estate,

yet

yet he wanted not Credit; and although he was baniſhed and forſaken by his own Friends and Countrymen, yet he was civilly received and relieved by ſtrangers, until God bleſs'd him,

Laſtly, With a happy return to his Native Country, his dear Children, and his own Eſtate; which although he found much ruined and broke, yet by his Prudence and Wiſdom, hath order'd as well as he could; and I hope, and pray God to add this bleſſing to all the reſt, That he may live long to encreaſe it for the benefit of his Poſterity.

6. Of his Honours and Dignities.

THe Honours, Titles and Dignities which were conferr'd upon my Lord, by King *James*, King *Charles* the Firſt, and King *Charles* the Second, partly as an encouragement for future Service, and a Reward for paſt, are following.

1. He was made Knight of the *Bath*, when he was but 15 or 16 years of Age, at the Creation of *Henry*, Prince of *Wales*, King *James's* Eldeſt Son.

2. King *James* Created him Viſcount *Mansfield*, and Baron of *Bolſover*.

3. King *Charles* the Firſt conſtituted him Lord Lieutenant of *Nottinghamſhire*, and

4. Lord

4. Lord Warden of the Forreſt of *Sherwood*; as alſo,

5. Lord Lieutenant of *Derby-ſhire.*

6. He choſe him Governour to His Son *Charles*, our now gracious King; and

7. Made him one of his Honourable Privy Council.

8. He conſtituted him Governour of the Town and County of *Newcaſtle*, and General of all His Majeſties Forces raiſed, and to be raiſed in the Northern parts of *England*; as alſo of the ſeveral Counties of *Nottingham, Lincoln, Rutland, Derby, Stafford, Leiceſter, Warwick, Northampton, Huntington, Cambridg, Norfolk, Suſſex, Eſſex* and *Hereford*, together with all the Appurtenances belonging to ſo great a Power, as is formerly declared.

9. He conferr'd upon him the Honour and Title of Earl of *Newcaſtle*, and Baron of *Bothal* and *Hepple.*

10. He created him Marqueſs of *Newcaſtle.*

11. His Majeſty King *CHARLES* the Second, was pleaſed, when my Lord was in baniſhment, to make him Knight of the moſt Noble Order of the Garter; And

12. After his Return into *England*, Chief Juſtice in *Eyre Trent-North.*

13. He created him Duke of *Newcaſtle*, and Earl of *Ogle.*

7. *Of the Entertainments He made for King* CHARLES *the First.*

THough my Lord hath alwayes been free and noble in his Entertainments and Feastings, yet he was pleased to shew his great Affection and Duty to his Gracious King, *Charles* the First, and Her Majesty the Queen, in some particular Entertainments which he made of purpose for them before the late Warrs.

When His Majesty was going into *Scotland* to be Crowned, he took His way through *Nottingham-shire*; and lying at *Worksop*-Mannor, hardly two miles distant from *Welbeck*, where my Lord then was, my Lord invited His Majesty thither to a Dinner, which he was graciously pleased to accept of: This Entertainment cost my Lord between Four and Five thousand pounds; which His Majesty liked so well, that a year after His Return out of *Scotland*, He was pleased to send my Lord word, That Her Majesty the Queen was resolved to make a Progress into the Northern parts, desiring him to prepare the like Entertainment for Her, as he had formerly done for Him: Which My Lord did, and endeavour'd for it with all possible Care and Industry, sparing nothing that might add splendor to that Feast, which both Their Majesties were pleased to honour with their Presence: *Ben Johnson* he employed in fitting such Scenes and Speeches as he could best devise; and sent for all the Gentry of the Country to come and wait on their Majesties; and in short, did all that ever he could imagine, to render it Great, and worthy Their Royal Acceptance.

This Entertainment he made at *Bolsover*-Castle in *Derbyshire*, some five miles distant from *Welbeck*, and resigned *Welbeck* for Their Majesties Lodging; it cost him in all between Fourteen and Fifteen thousand pounds.

Besides these two, there was another small Entertainment which my Lord prepared for His late Majesty, in his own Park at *Welbeck*, when His Majesty came down, with his two Nephews, the now Prince Elector Palatine, and His Brother Prince *Rupert*, into the Forrest of *Sherwood*; which cost him Fifteen hundred pounds.

And this I mention not out of a vain-glory, but to declare the great love and Duty, my Lord had for His Gracious King and Queen, and to correct the mistakes committed by some Historians, who not being rightly informed of those Entertainments, make the World believe Falshood for Truth. But as I said, they were made before the Warrs, when my Lord had the possessiou of a great Estate, and wanted nothing to express his Love and Duty to his Soveraign in that manner; whereas now he should be

much

much to feek to do the like, his Eftate being fo much
ruined by the late Civil Wars, that neither himfelf nor
his Pofterity will be able fo foon to recover it.

8. *His Education.*

HIs Education was according to his Birth; for
as he was born a Gentleman, fo he was bred like
a Gentleman.   To School-Learning he never fhew'd
a great inclination; for though he was fent to the U-
niverfity, and was a Student of St. *John's* Colledg in
Cambridg, and had his Tutors to inftruct him; yet
they could not perfwade him to read or ftudy much,
he taking more delight in fports, then in learning; fo
that his Father being a wife man, and feeing that his
Son had a good natural Wit, and was of a very good
Difpofition, fuffer'd him to follow his own Genius;
whereas his other Son *Charles*, in whom he found a
greater love and inclination to Learning, he encou-
raged as much that way, as poffibly he could.

One time it hapned that a young Gentleman, one
of my Lord's Relations, had bought fome Land, at the
fame time when my Lord had bought a *Singing-Boy*
for 50 l. a Horfe for 50 l. and a Dog for 2 l. which
humour his Father Sir *Charles* liked fo well, that he was
pleafed to fay, That if he fhould find his Son to be fo covetous, that he would buy Land before he was 20 years

O o   of

of Age, he would difinherit him. But above all
the reft, my Lord had a great inclination to the
Art of Horfemanfhip and Weapons, in which later,
his Father Sir *Charles*, being a moft ingenuous and un-
parallell'd Mafter of that Age, was his onely Tutor,
and kept him alfo feveral Mafters in the Art of Horfemanfhip, and fent him to the *Mewfe* to *Monf. An-*
toine, who was then accounted the beft Mafter in that
Art. But my Lord's delight in thofe Heroick Exer-
cifes was fuch, that he foon became Mafter thereof
Himfelf, which encreafed much his Father's hopes of
his future perfections, who being himfelf a perfon of a
Noble and Heroick nature, was extreamly well pleafed
to obferve his Son take delight in fuch Arts and Exer-
cifes as were proper and fit for a perfon of Quality.

9. *His Natural Wit and Underftanding.*

ALthough my Lord has not fo much of Scholar-
fhip and Learning as his Brother Sir *Charles Ca-*
vendifh had, yet he hath an excellent Natural Wit
and Judgment, and dives into the bottom of every
thing; as it is evidently apparent in the forementio-
ned Art of Horfemanfhip and Weapons, which by
his own ingenuity he has reformed and brought to fuch
perfection, as never any one has done heretofore: And
though he is no Mathematician by Art, yet he hath a
                                                    very

very good Mathematical brain, to demonſtrate Truth
by natural reaſon, and is both a good Natural and
Moral Philoſopher, not by reading Philoſophical
Books, but by his own Natural Underſtanding and
Obſervation, by which he hath found out many
Truths.

To paſs by ſeveral other inſtances, I'le but mention,
that when my Lord was at *Paris*, in his Exile, it happen'd one time, that he diſcourſing with ſome of his
Friends, amongſt whom was alſo that Learned Philoſopher *Hobbes*, they began amongſt the reſt, to argue
upon this ſubject, namely, *Whether it were poſſible to
make Man by Art fly as Birds do*; and when ſome of the
Company had delivered their Opinion, *viz.* That
they thought it probable to be done by the help of Ar-
tificial Wings : My Lord declared, that he deemed
it altogether impoſſible, and demonſtrared it by this
following Reaſon : Man's Armes, ſaid he, are not
ſet on his ſhoulders in the ſame manner as Bird's wings
are; for that part of the Arm which joins to the Shoul-
der, is in Man placed inward, as towards the breaſt,
but in Birds outward, as toward the back ; which
difference and contrary poſition or ſhape, hinders that
man cannot have the ſame flying-action with his Armes,
as Birds have with their Wings; Which Argument
Mr. *Hobbes* liked ſo well, that he was pleaſed to make
uſe of it in one of his Books called *Leviathan*, if I remember well.

                                      Some

Some other time they falling into a Discourse concerning Witches, Mr. *Hobbes* said, That though he could not rationally believe there were Witches, yet he could not be fully satisfied to believe there were none, by reason they would themselves confess it, if strictly examined.

To which my Lord answer'd, That though for his part he cared not whether there were Witches or no; yet his Opinion was, That the Confession of Witches, and their suffering for it, proceeded from an Erroneous Belief, *viz*. That they had made a Contract with the Devil to serve him for such Rewards as were in his Power to give them; and that it was their Religion to worship and adore him; in which Religion they had such a firm and constant belief, that if any thing came to pass according to their desire, they believed the Devil had heard their prayers, and granted their requests, for which they gave him thanks; but if things fell out contrary to their prayers and desires, then they were troubled at it, fearing they had offended him, or not served him as they ought, and asked him forgiveness for their offences. Also (said my Lord) they imagine that their Dreams are real exterior actions; for example, if they dream they flye in the Air, or out of the Chimney top, or that they are turned into several shapes, they believe no otherwise, but that it is really so: And this wicked Opinion makes them in-

induftrious to perform fuch Ceremonies to the Devil, that they adore and worfhip him as their God,
and chufe to live and dye for him.

Thus my Lord declared himfelf concerning Witches, which Mr. *Hobbes* was alfo pleafed to infert in
his fore-mentioned Book: But yet my Lord doth
not count this Opinion of his fo univerfal, as if
there were none but imaginary Witches; for he doth
not fpeak but of fuch a fort of Witches as make it
their Religion to worfhip the Devil in the manner a-
forefaid. Nor doth he think it a Crime to entertain
what Opinion feems moft probable to him, in things
indifferent; for in fuch cafes men may difcourfe and
argue as they pleafe, to exercife their Wit, and
may change and alter their Opinions upon more
probable Grounds and Reafons; whereas in Funda-
mental matters both of Church and State, he is fo
ftrict an Adherent to them, that he will never maintain or defend fuch Opinions which are in the leaft
prejudicial to either.

One proof more I'le add to confirm his Natural
Underftanding and Judgment, which was upon
fome Difcourfe I held with him one time, concerning
that famous Chymift *Van Helmont*, who in his Writings is very invective againft the School-men, and
amongft the reft, accufes them for taking the Radical moifture for the fat of Animal Bodies. Whereupon my Lord anfwer'd, That furely the School-

men were too wife to commit fuch an Error; for
faid he, the Radical moifture is not the fat or
tallow of an Animal, but an Oily and Balfamous
Subftance; for the fat and tallow, as alfo the watery
parts, are cold; whereas the Oily and Balfamous
parts, have at all times a lively heat; which makes
that thofe Creatures which have much of that Oyle
or Balfom, are long-liv'd, and appear young; and
not onely Animals, but alfo Vegetables, which
have much of that Oyle or Balfom, as Ivy, Bayes,
Laurel, Holly, and the like, live long, and appear
frefh and green, not onely in Winter, but when
they are old. Then I ask'd my Lord's Opinion concerning the Radical heat: To which he anfwer'd,
That the Radical heat lived in the Radical moifture;
and when the one decayed, the other decayed alfo; and
then was produced either an unnatural heat, which caufed an unnatural drynefs; or an unnatural moifture,
which caufed Dropfies, and thefe, an unnatural cold-
nefs.

Laftly; His Natural Wit appears by his delight
in Poetry; for I may juftly call him the beft *Lyrick*
and *Dramatick* Poet of this Age: His Comedies do
fufficiently fhew his great Obfervation and Judgment,
for they are compofed of thefe three Ingredients, *viz*.
Wit, Humour and *Satyre*; and his chief Defign in
them, is to divulge and laugh at the follies of Mankind; to perfecute Vice, and to encourage Virtue.

10. *Of*

Book III.   DUKE *of* NEWCASTLE.   147

10. *Of his Natural Humour and Disposition.*

MY Lord may juſtly be compared to *Titus* the *Deliciæ* of Mankind, by reaſon of his ſweet, gentle and obliging Nature; for though his Wiſdom and Experience found it impoſſible to pleaſe all men, becauſe of their different humours and diſpoſitions; yet his Nature is ſuch, that he will be ſorry when he ſeeth that men are diſpleaſed with him out of their own ill Natures, without any cauſe; for he loves all that are his Friends, and hates none that are his Enemies: He is a Loyal Subject, a kind Husband, a Loving Father, a Generous Maſter, and a Conſtant Friend.

His natural Love to his Parents has been ſo great, that I have heard him ſay, he would moſt willingly, and without the leſt repining, have begg'd for his daily relief, ſo God would but have let his Parents live.

He is true and juſt both in his words and actions, and has no mean or petty Deſigns, but they are all juſt and honeſt.

He condemns not upon Report, but upon Proof; nor judges by Words, but Actions; he forgets not paſt Service, for preſent Advantage; but gives a preſent Reward to a preſent Deſert.

He hath a great Power over his Paſſions, and hath had the greateſt tryals thereof; for certainly He muſt

of

of neceſſity have a great ſhare of Patience, that can forgive ſo many falſe, treacherous, malicious and ungrateful Perſons as he hath done; but he is ſo wiſe, that his Paſſion never out-runs his Patience, nor his Extravagancies his Prudence; and although his Private Enemies have been numerous, yet I verily believe, there is never a ſubject more generally beloved then He is.

He hates Pride and loves Humility; is civil to Strangers, kind to his Acquaintance, and reſpectful to all perſons, according to their Quality; He never regards Place, except it be for Ceremony: To the meaneſt perſon he'll put off his Hat, and ſuffer every body to ſpeak to him.

He never refuſes any Petition, but accepts them; and being informed of the buſineſs, will give a juſt, and as much as lies in him, a favourable anſwer to the Petitioning Party.

He eaſily Pardons, and bountifully Rewards; and always praiſes particular mens Virtues, but covers their Faults with ſilence.

He is full of Charity and Compaſſion to perſons that are in miſery, and full of Clemency and Mercy; in ſo much, that when he was General of a great Army, he would never ſit in Council himſelf upon Cauſes of Life and Death, but granted Pardon to many Delinquents that were condemned by his Council of War; ſo that ſome were forced to Petition him not

to

to do it, by reafon it was an ill prefident for others. To which my Lord merrily anfwer'd , That if they did hang all, they would leave him none to fight.

His Courage he always fhew'd in Action, more then in Words, for he would Fight, but not Rant.

He is not Vain-glorious to heighten or brag of his Heroick Actions ; Witnefs that great Victory upon *Atherton-moor*, after which he would not fuffer his Trumpets to found, but came quietly and filently into the City of *York*, for which he would certainly have been blamed by thofe that make a great noife upon fmall caufes ; and love to be applauded, though their actions little deferve it.

His noble Bounty and Generofity is fo manifeft to all the World, that I fhould light a Candle to the Sun, if I fhould ftrive to illuftrate it ; for he has no felf-defigns or felf-intereft, but will rather wrong and injure himfelf then others. To give you but one proof of this noble Vertue, it is known, that where he hath a legal right to Felons Goods, as he hath in a great part of his Eftate, yet he never took or exacted more then fome inconfiderable fhare for acknowledgment of his Right ; faying, That he was refolved never to grow rich by other mens misfortunes.

In fhort, I know him not addicted to any manner of Vice, except that he has been a great lover and admirer of the Female Sex ; which whether it be fo great

Q q   a

a crime as to condemn him for it ; I'le leave to the
judgment of young Gallants and beautiful La-
dies.

11. *Of His outward Shape and Behaviour.*

HIs Shape is neat, and exactly proportioned; his
Stature of a middle size, and his Complexion
sanguine.

His Behaviour is such, that it might be a Pattern
for all Gentlemen ; for it is Courtly, Civil, easie and
free, without Formality or Constraint; and yet hath
something in it of grandure, that causes an awful respect
towards him.

12. *Of His Discourse.*

HIs Discourse is as free and unconcerned, as his Behaviour, Pleasant, Witty, and Instructive;
He is quick in Reparties or sudden answers, and hates
dubious disputes, and premeditated Speeches. He
loves also to intermingle his Discourse with some
short pleasant stories, and witty sayings, and always
names the Author from whom he hath them ; for he
hates to make another man's Wit his own.

13. *Of His* HABIT.

HE accouters his Perſon according to the Faſhi-
on, if it be one that is not troubleſome and
uneaſie for men of Heroick Exerciſes and Actions.
He is neat and cleanly; which makes him to be ſome-
what long in dreſſing, though not ſo long as many
effeminate perſons are. He ſhifts ordinarily once a
day, and every time when he uſes Exerciſe, or his
temper is more hot then ordinary.

---

14. *Of His* DIET.

IN his Diet he is ſo ſparing and temperate, that he
never eats nor drinks beyond his ſet proportion,
ſo as to ſatisfie onely his natural appetite: He makes but
one Meal a day, at which he drinks two good Glaſ-
ſes of Small-Beer, one about the beginning, the other
at the end thereof, and a little Glaſs of Sack in the
middle of his Dinner; which Glaſs of Sack he alſo
uſes in the morning for his Breakfaſt, with a Morſel
of Bread. His Supper conſiſts of an Egg, and a
draught of Small-beer. And by this Temperance
he finds himſelf very healthful, and may yet live many

ny years, he being now of the Age of Seventy
three, which I pray God from my foul, to grant him.

15. H*is Recreation and Exercife.*

HIS prime Paftime and Recreation hath always
been the Exercife of Mannage and Weapons;
which Heroick Arts he ufed to practife every day;
but I obferving that when he had over-heated himfelf, he would be apt to take cold, prevail'd fo far,
that at laft he left the frequent ufe of the Mannage,
ufing neverthelefs ftill the Exercife of Weapons ;
and though he doth not ride himfelf fo frequently as
he hath done; yet he takes delight in feeing his Horfes of Mannage rid by his Efcuyers, whom he in-
ftructs in that Art for his own pleafure. But in the
Art of Weapons (in which he has a method beyond
all that ever were famous in it, found out by his
own Ingenuity and Practice) he never taught any
body, but the now Duke of *Buckingham*, whofe
Guardian He hath been, and his own two Sons.

The reft of his time he fpends in Mufick, Poetry, Architecture and the like.

16. *His*

16. *Of His Pedigree.*

HAving made promise in the beginning of the first Book, that I would join a more large Description of the Pedigree of my Noble Lord and Husband, to the end of the History of his life: I shall now discharge my self; and though I could derive it from a longer time, and reckon up a great many of his Ancestors, even from the time of *William* the Conqueror, He being descended from the most ancient family of the *Gernouns*, as *Cambden* relates in his *Britannia*, in the Description of *Derbyshire*; yet it being a work fitter for Heralds, I shall proceed no further then his Grandfather, and shew you onely those noble Families which my Lord is allied to by his Birth.

My Lord's Grandfather, by his Father, (as is formerly mentioned) was Sir *William Cavendish*, Privy-Counsellor and Treasurer of the Chamber to King *Henry* the Eighth, *Edward* the Sixth, and Queen *Mary*; who married two Wives; by the first he had onely two Daughters; but by the second, *Elizabeth*, who was my Lords Grandmother, he had three Sons and four Daughters, whereof one Daughter died young. She was Daughter to *John Hardwick* of *Hardwick*, in the County of *Derby*, Esq; and had four Husbands: The first was — *Barlow* Esq; who died before they were bedded together, they being both very young. The

R r   second

second was Sir *William Cavendish*, my Lord's Grandfather, who being somewhat in years, married her
chiefly for her beauty ; she had so much power in his
affection, that she perswaded him to sell his Estate which
he had in the Southern parts of *England* (for he was
very rich) and buy an Estate in the Northern parts,
viz. in *Derbyshire*, and thereabout, where her own
friends and kindred liv'd, which he did ; and having
there setled himself, upon her further perswasion, built
a Mannor-house in the same County, call'd *Chattes-
worth*, which, as I have heard, cost first and last a-
bove 80000 l. *sterling*. But before this House was
finish'd, he died, and left six Children , *viz.* three
Sons and three Daughters, which before they came to
be marriageable , she married a third Husband, Sir
William St *Loo* Captain of the Guard to Queen *Elizabeth*, and Grand Butler of *England*; who dying without Issue, she married a fourth Husband, *George* Earl
of *Shrewsbury*, by whom she left no Issue.

The Children which she had by her second Husband, Sir *William Cavendish*, being grown marriageable ; the eldest Son *Henry*, married *Grace* the young-
est Daughter of his Father in Law, the said *George*
Earl of *Shrewsbury*, which he had by his former Wife
Gertrude, Daughter of *Thomas Manners*, Earl of *Rutland*, but died without Issue.

The second Son *William*, after Earl of *Devonshire*,
had two Wives ; the first was an Heiress, by whom he
had

had Children, but all died save one Son, whose name was also *William*, Earl of *Devonshire* : His second Wife was Widdow to Sir *Edward Wortly*, who had several Children by her first Husband, and but one Son by the said *Will. Cavendish*, after Earl of *Devonshire*, who dyed young.

His Son by his first Wife, (*William* Earl of *Devonshire*) married *Christian*, Daughter of *Edward* Lord *Bruce*, a *Scots*-man, by whom he had two Sons, and one Daughter; the Eldest Son *William*, now Earl of *Devonshire*, married *Elizabeth*, the second Daughter of *William* Earl of *Salisbury*, by whom he has three children, *viz.* Two Sons and one Daughter, whereof the Eldest Son *William* is married to the second Daughter of *James* now Duke of *Ormond*; the second Son *Charles* is yet a youth: The Daughter *Anne* married the Lord *Rich*, the onely Son and Child to *Charles* now Earl of *Warwick*; but he dyed without Issue.

The second Son of *William* Earl of *Devonshire*, and Brother to the now Earl of *Devonshire*, was unfortunately slain in the late Civil Warrs, as is before mentioned.

The Daughter of the said *William* Earl of *Devonshire*, Sister to the now Earl of *Devonshire*, married *Robert* Lord *Rich*, Eldest Son to *Robert* Earl of *Warwick*, by whom she had but one Son, who married, but dyed without Issue.

The

The third and youngeſt Son of Sir *William Ca-*
vendiſh, Charles Cavendiſh, (my Lord's Father) had
two Wives; the firſt was Daughter and Coheir to
Sir *Thomas Kidſon,* who dyed a year after her Marriage, without iſſue: The ſecond was the younger
Daughter of *Cuthbert* Lord *Ogle,* and after her Elder and onely Siſter *Jane,* Wife to *Edward Earl* of
Shrewsbury, who dyed without Iſſue, became Heir
to her Father's Eſtate and Title; by whom he had
three Sons; whereof the eldeſt dyed in his Infancy;
the ſecond was *William,* my dear Lord and Huſ-
band; the third, *Charles,* who dyed a Batchelour
about the age of Sixty three.

My Lord hath had two Wives; the firſt was *E-*
lizabeth, Daughter and Heir to *William Baſſet* of
Bloore, in the County of *Stafford,* Eſq; and Widow
to *Henry Howard,* younger Son to *Thomas* Earl
of *Suffolk;* by whom he had ten Children, *viz.* ~~Five~~ 6
Sons, and ~~five~~ ⁴Daughters; whereof five, *viz.* ~~three~~ 4
Sons, and ~~two~~ ᵒⁿˢ Daughter, dyed young; the reſt,
viz. Two Sons and three Daughters, came to be
married.

His Elder Son, *Charles,* Viſcount of *Mansfield,*
married the Eldeſt Daughter and Heir of Mr. *Ri-*
chard Rogers, by whom he had but one Daughter,
who dyed ſoon after her birth; and he dyed alſo without any other Iſſue.

His ſecond Son *Henry,* now Earl of *Ogle,* married

ried *Francis* the eldeſt Daughter of Mr. *William Pier-repont*, by whom he hath had three Sons, and four Daughters; two Sons were born before their narural time; the third, *Henry* Lord *Mansfield* is alive: The four Daughters are, the Lady *Elizabeth*, Lady *Frances*, Lady *Margaret*, and Lady *Catharine*.

My Lords three Daughters were thus married; The eldeſt, Lady *Jane*, married *Charles Cheiney*, Eſq; deſcended of a very noble and ancient Family; by whom ſhe hath one Son and two Daughters. The ſecond, Lady *Elizabeth*, married *John* now Earl of *Bridgwater*, then Lord *Brackly*, and eldeſt Son to *John* then Earl of *Bridgwater*; who died in Childbed, and left five Sons, and one Daughter, whereof the eldeſt Son *John* Lord *Brackly*, married the Lady *Elizabeth*, onely Daughter and Child to *James* then Earl of *Middleſex*.

My Lords third Daughter, the Lady *Frances*, married *Oliver* Earl of *Bullingbrook*, and hath had no Child yet.

After the death of my Lords firſt Wife, who died the 17*th* of *April*, in the Year 1643, he married me, *Margaret*, Daughter to *Thomas Lucas* of St. *Johns* near *Colcheſter*, in *Eſſex*, Eſquire; but hath no Iſſue by me.

And this is the Poſterity of the three Sons of Sir *William Cavendiſh*, my Lords Grandfather by his Fathers ſide; The three Daughters were diſpoſed of as followeth: S ſ   The

The eldeſt, *Frances Cavendiſh*, married Sir *Henry Pierrepont* of *Holm Pierrepont*, in the County of *Nottingham*, by whom ſhe had two Sons, whereof the firſt died young ; The ſecond, *Robert*, after Earl of *Kingſton* upon *Hull*, married *Gertrude*, the eldeſt Daughter, and Co-heir to *Henry Talbot*, fourth Son to *George* Earl of *Shrewsbury*, by whom he had five Sons and three Daughters, whereof the eldeſt Son, *Henry*, now Marqueſs of *Dorcheſter*, hath had two Wives; the firſt *Cecilia*, Eldeſt Daughter to the Lord Viſcount *Bayning*, by whom he had ſeveral Children, of which there are living onely two Daughters ; the eldeſt *Anne*, who married *John Roſſe*, onely Son to *John* now Earl of *Rutland*; the ſecond, *Grace*, who is unmarried. His ſecond Wife was *Catharine*, ſecond Daughter to *James* Earl of *Derby*, by whom he has no Iſſue living.

The ſecond Son of the Earl of *Kingſton*, *William*, married the ſole Daughter and Heir of Sir *Thomas Harries*, by whom he had Iſſue five Sons, and five Daughters, whereof two Sons and two Daugters died unmarried : The other ſix are,

Robert the Eldeſt, who married *Elizabeth*, Daughter and Co-heir to Sir *John Evelyne*, by whom he has three Sons, and one Daughter. The ſecond Son *George*, and the third *Gervas*, are yet unmarried.

The eldeſt Daughter of *William Pierrepont*, *Frances*, is married to my Lords now onely Son and Heir, *Henry* Earl of *Ogle*, as before is mentioned.

The

The second, *Grace*, is married to *Gilbert* now Earl of *Clare*, by whom he hath Iſſue, Two ſons, and three daughters.

The third, *Gertrude*, is unmarried.

The third ſon of the Earl of *Kingſton*, *Francis Pierrepont*, married *Elizabeth* the eldeſt daughter of Mr. *Bray*, by whom he had Iſſue, one ſon, and one daughter; the ſon, *Robert*, married *Anne* the daughter of *Henry Murray*. The daughter, *Frances*, married *William Pagatt*, eldeſt ſon to *William* Lord *Pagatt*.

The fourth ſon of the Earl of *Kingſton*, *Gervaſe*, is unmarried.

The fifth ſon, *George Pierrepont*, married the daughter of Mr. *Jonas*, by whom he had two ſons unmarried, *Henry* and *Samuel*.

The three daughters of the ſaid Earl of *Kingſton*, are, *Frances* the eldeſt, who was married to *Philip Rowleſton*; the ſecond, *Mary*, dyed young; the third, *Elizabeth*, is unmarried.

The ſecond daughter of Sir *William Cavendiſh*, *Elizabeth*, married the Earl of *Lennox*, Unkle to King *James*; by whom ſhe had onely one daughter, the Lady *Arabella*, who againſt King *Jame*'s Commands (ſhe being after Him and His Children, the next Heir to the Crown) married *William*, the ſecond ſon to the Earl of *Hereford*; for which ſhe was put into the Tower, where not long after ſhe dyed.

The

The youngeſt daughter *Mary Cavendiſh*, marri-
èd *Glbert Talbot*, ſecond ſon to *George* Earl of *Shrewsbury*; who after the deceaſe of his Father, and his
elder Brother *Francis*, who dyed without Iſſue, became Earl of *Shrewsbury*; by whom ſhe had Iſſue,
foꝛ ſons, and three daughters; the ſons all dyed in
their Infancy, but the daughters were married.

The eldeſt, *Mary Talbot*, married *William* Her-
bert, Earl of *Pembroke*, by whom (ſome eighteen
years after her Marriage) ſhe had one ſon, who dyed young.

The ſecond daughter, *Elizabeth*, married Sir Henry *Gray*, after *Earl* of *Kent*, (the fourth Earl of
England) by whom ſhe had no Iſſue.

The third and youngeſt daughter *Aletheia*, married *Thomas Howard* Earl of *Arundel*, the firſt Earl,
and Earl-Marſhal of *England*; by whom ſhe left two
ſons, *James*, who died beyond the ſeas without Iſſue;
and *Henry*, who married *Elizabeth*, daughter of *Eſme
Stuart*, Duke of *Lennox*; by whom he had Iſſue, ſeveral ſons, and one daughter; whereof the eldeſt ſon,
Thomas, (ſince the Reſtauration of King *Charles* the
Second) was reſtored to the Dignity of his Ance-
ſtors, *viz.* Duke of *Norfolk*, next to the Royal
Family, the firſt Duke of *England*.

And this is briefly the Pedigree of my dear Lord
and Husband, from his Grandfather by his Fathers
ſide:

fide; concerning his Kindred and alliances by his Mother, who was *Katherine,* Daughter to *Cuthbert* Lord *Ogle*, they are so many, that it is impossible for me to enumerate them all, My Lord being by his Mother related to the chief of the most ancient Families of *Northumberland,* and other the Northern parts; onely this I may mention, that My Lord is a Peer of the Realm, from the first year of King *Edward* the Fourth his Reign.

Tt   THE

THE FOURTH
B O O K:

Containing feveral

Eſſays and Diſcourſes

Gather'd from the Mouth of

MY NOBLE LORD and HUSBAND.

With ſome few Notes of mine own.

I have heard My Lord ſay,

I.

THat thoſe which command the Wealth of a Kingdom, command the hearts and hands of the People.

II.

That He is a great Monarch, who hath a Soveraign Command over Church, Laws and Armes; and He a wiſe Monarch, that imploys his ſubjects for their own profit, (for their profit is his) encourages Tradeſmen, and aſſiſts and defends Merchants.

III.

That it is a part of Prudence in a Commonwealth or Kingdom to encourage drayners; for drowned Lands are

are onely fit to maintain and encreafe fome wild Ducks, whereas being drained, they are able to afford nourifhment and food to Cattel, befides the producing of feveral forts of Fruit and Corn.

IV.

That without a well order'd force, a Prince doth but reign upon the courtefie of others.

V.

That great Princes fhould not fuffer their chief Cities to be ftronger then themfelves.

VI.

That great Princes are half-armed, when their fubjects are unarmed, unlefs it be in time of Foreign Wars.

VII.

That that Prince is richeft, who is Mafter of the Purfe; and he ftrongeft that is Mafter of the Armes; and he wifeft that can tell how to fave the one, and ufe the other.

VIII.

That Great Princes fhould be the onely Pay-Mafters of their Soldiers, and pay them out of their own Treafuries; for all men follow the Purfe; and fo they'l have both the Civil and Martial Power in their hands.

IX.

That Great Monarchs fhould rather ftudy men, then Books; for all affairs or bufinefs are amongft Men.

X.

X.

That a Prince should advance Foreign Trade or Traffick to the utmost of his Power, because no State or Kingdom can be Rich without it; and where Subjects are poor, the Soveraign can have but little.

X I.

That Trade and Traffick brings Honey to the Hive; that is to say, Riches to the Commonwealth; whereas other Professions are so far from that, that they rather rob the Commonwealth, instead of enriching it.

XII.

That it is not so much unseasonable Weather that makes the Countrey complain of Scarcity, but want of Commerce; for whensoever Commodities are cheap, it is a sign that Commerce is decayed; because the cheapness of them, shews a scarcity of money; for example, put the case five men came to Market to buy a Horse, and each of them had no more but ten pounds, the Seller can receive no more then what the Buyer has, but must content himself with those ten pounds, if he be necessitated to sell his Horse: But if each one of the Buyers had an hundred pounds to lay out for a Horse, the Seller might receive as much. Thus Commodities are cheap or dear, according to the plenty or scarcity of money; and though we had Mynes of Gold and Silver at home, and no Traffick into Foreign parts, yet we

should

should want neceffaries from other Nations, which
proves that no Nation can live or fubfift well, without Foreign Trade and Commerce ; for God and
Nature have order'd it fo , That no particular Nation is provided with all things.

XIII.

That Merchants by carrying out more Commodities then they bring in ; that is to fay, by felling
more then they buy, do enrich a State or Kingdom
with money, that hath none in its own bowels ; but
what Kingdom or State foever hath Mynes of Gold
and Silver , there Merchants buy more then they fell,
to furnifh and accommodate it with neceffary provifions.   XIV.

That debafing, and fetting a higher value upon
money, is but a prefent fhift of poor and needy
Princes; and doth more hurt for the future, then
good for the prefent.

XV.

That Foraign Commerce caufes frequent Voyages; and frequent Voyages make skilful and experienced Sea-men, and Skilful Seamen are a Brazen Wall
to an Ifland.

XVI.

That he is the Powerfulleft Monarch that hath the
beft fhipping; and that a Prince fhould hinder his
Neighbours as much as he can, from being ftrong at
Sea.

U u

XVII.

XVII.

That wife States-men ought to underſtand the Laws, Cuſtomes and Trade of the Commonwealth, and have good intelligence both of Foraign Tranſa-ctions and Deſigns, and of Domeſtick Factions; alſo they ought to have a Treaſury, and well-fur-niſhed Magazine.

XVIII.

That it is a great matter in a *State* or Kingdom, to take care of the Education of Youth, to breed them ſo, that they may know firſt how to obey, and then how to command and order affairs wiſely.

XIX.

That it is great Wiſdom in a State, to breed and train up good States-men: As, firſt, To let them be ſome time at the Univerſities: Next, To put them to the Innes of Court, that they may have ſome knowledg of the Laws of the Land; then to ſend them to travel with ſome Ambaſſador, in the quali-ty of Secretary; and let them be Agents or Reſi-dents in Foraign Countreys. Fourthly, To make them Clerks of the Signet, or Council: And laſtly, To make them Secretaries of State, or give them ſome other Employment in State-Affairs.

XX.

That there ſhould be more Praying, and leſs Preaching; for much Preaching breeds Faction; but much Praying cauſes Devotion.

XXI. That

XXI.

That young people fhould be frequently Catechi-fed, and that Wife Men rather then Learned, fhould be chofen heads of Schools and Colledges.

XXII.

That the more divifions there are in Church and State, the more trouble and confufion is apt to enfue: Wherefore too many Controverfies and Difputes in the one, and too many Law-Cafes and Pleadings in the other ought to be avoided and fuppreffed.

XXIII.

That Difputes and Factions amongft States-men, are fore-runners of future diforders, if not total ruines.

XXIV.

That all Books of Controverfies fhould be writ in Latin, that none but the Learned may read them, and that there fhould be no Difputations but in Schools, left it breed Factions amongft the Vulgar; for Difputations and Controverfies are a kind of Civil War, maintained by the Pen, and often draw out the fword foon after; Alfo that all Prayer-Books fhould be writ in the native Language; that Excommunications fhould not be too frequent for every little and petty trefpafs; that every Clergy-man fhould be kind and loving to his Parifhioners, not proud and quarrel-fome.

XXV.

That Ceremony is nothing in it self, and yet doth every thing; for without Ceremony there would be no diftinction neither in Church nor State.

XXVI.

That Orders and Profeffions ought not to entrench upon each other, left in time they make a confufion a-mongft themfelves.

XXVII.

That in a Well-ordered State or Covernment, care fhould be taken left any degree or profeffion what-foever fwell too big, or grow too numerous, it being not onely a hinderance to thofe of the fame profeffion, but a burden to the Commonwealth, which cannot be well if it exceeds in extreams.

XXVIII.

That the Taxes fhould not be above the riches of the Commonwealth, for that muft upon neceffity breed Factions and Civil Wars, by reafon a general poverty united, is far more dangerous then a private Purfe; for though their Wealth be fmall, yet their Unity and Combination makes them ftrong; fo that being armed with neceffity, they become outragious with defpair.

XXIX.

That Heavy Taxes upon Farmes, ruine the Nobi-lity and Gentry; for if the Tenant be poor, the Land-lord

lord cannot be rich, he having nothing but his Rents to live on.

XXX.

That it is not fo much Laws and Religion, nor Rhetorick, that keeps a State or Kingdom in order, but Armes; which if they be not imploy'd to an evil ufe, keep up the right and priviledges both of Crown, Church and State.

XXXI.

That no equivocations fhould be ufed either in Church or Law; for the one caufes feveral Opinions to the difturbance of mens Confciences; the other long and tedious Suits, to the difturbance of mens private Affairs; and both do oftentimes ruine and impoverifh the State.

XXXII.

That in Cafes of Robberies and Murthers, it is better to be fevere, then merciful; for the hanging of a few, will fave the lives and Purfes of many.

XXXIII.

That many Laws do rather entrap, then help the fubject.

XXXIV.

That no Martial Law fhould be executed, but in an Army.

XXXV.

That the Sheriffs in this Kingdom of *England* have been fo expenfive in Liveries and Entertainments in

X x   the

the time of their Sherifalty, as it hath ruined many
Families that had but indifferent Eftates.

XXXVI.

That the cutting down of Timber in the time of Rebellion, has been an ineftimable lofs to this Kingdom,
by reafon of Shipping ; for though Timber might be
had out of Foreign Countries that would ferve for
the building of Ships, yet there is none of fuch a temper as our *Englifh* Oak ; it being not onely ftrong
and large, but not apt to fplint, which renders the
Ships of other Nations much inferior to ours ; and
that therefore it would be very beneficial for the
Kingdom, to fet out fome Lands for the bearing of
fuch Oaks, by fowing of Acorns, and then tranf-
planting them ; which would be like a Store-houfe for
fhipping, and bring an incomparable benefit to the
Kingdom, fince in Shipping confifts our greateft
ftrength, they being the onely Walls that defend an
Ifland.

XXXVII.

That the Nobility and Gentry in this Kingdom,
have done themfelves a great injury, by giving away
(out of a petty pride) to the Commonalty, the power of being Juries and Juftices of Peace ; for certainly they cannot but underftand, that that muft of neceffity be an act of great Confequence and Power,
which concerns mens Lives, Lands and Eftates.

XXXVIII. That

XXXVIII.

That it is no act of Prudence to make poor and mean persons Governours or Commanders, either by Land or Sea; by reason their poverty causes them to take Bribes, and so betray their Trust; at best, they are apt to extort, which is a great grievance to the people; besides, it breeds envy in the Nobility and Gentry, who by that means rise into Factions, and cause disturbances in a State or Commonwealth: Wherefore the best way is to chuse Rich and Honourable Persons, (or at least, Gentlemen) for such Employments, who esteem Fame and Honourable Actions, above their Lives; and if they want skill, they must get such under-Officers as have more then themselves, to instruct them.

XXXIX.

That great Princes should consider, before they make War against Foreign Nations, whether they be able to maintain it; for if they be not able, then it is better to submit to an honourable Peace, then to make Warr to their great disadvantage; but if they be able to maintain Warr, then they'l force (in time) their Enemies to submit and yeild to what Tearms and Conditions they please.

XL.

That, when a State or Government is ensnarled and troubled, it is more easie to raise the common people to a Factious Mutiny, then to draw them to a Loyal Duty.   XLI. That

XLI.

That in a Kingdom where Subjects are apt to rebel, no Offices or Commands should be sold; for those that buy, will not onely use extortion, and practise unjust wayes to make out their purchase, but be ablest to rebel, by reason they are more for private gain, then the publick good; for it is probable their Principles are like their Purchases.

But, that all Magistrates, Officers, Commanders, Heads and Rulers, in what Profession soever, both in Church and State, should be chosen according to their Abilities, Wisdom, Courage, Piety, Justice, Honesty and Loyalty; and then they'l mind the publick Good, more then their particular Interest.

XLII.

That those which have Politick Designs, are for the most part dishonest, by reason their Designs tend more to Interest, then Justice.

XLIII.

That Great Princes should onely have Great, Noble and Rich Persons to attend them, whose Purses and Power may alwayes be ready to assist them.

XLIV.

That a Poor Nobility is apt to be Factious; and a Numerous Nobility is a burden to a Commonwealth.

XLV.

XLV.

That in a Monarchical Government, to be for the King, is to be for the Commonwealth; for when Head and Body are divided, the Life of Happiness dies, and the Soul of Peace is departed.

XLVI.

That, as it is a great Error in a State to have all Affairs put into *Gazettes*, (for it over-heats the peoples brains, and makes them neglect their private Affairs, by over-busying themselves with State-business;) so it is great Wisdom for a Council of State to have good Intelligences (although they be bought with great Cost and Charges) as well of Domestick, as Foreign Affairs and Transactions, and to keep them in private for the benefit of the Commonwealth.

XLVII.

That there is no better Policy for a Prince to please his People, then to have many Holy-dayes for their ease, and order several Sports and Pastimes for their Recreation, and to be himself sometime Spectator thereof; by which means he'l not onely gain love and respect from the people, but busie their minds in harmless actions, sweeten their Natures, and hinder them from Factious Designs.

XLVIII.

That it is more difficult and dangerous for a Prince or Commander to raise an Army in such a time when the Countrey is embroiled in a Civil Warr, then to lead out an Army to fight a Battel; for when an Army is raifed, he hath ftrength; but in raifing it, he hath none.

XLIX.

That good Commanders, and experienced Soldiers, are like skilfull Fencers, who defend with Prudence, and affault with Courage, and kill their Enemies by Art, not trufting their Lives to Chance or Fortune; for as a little man with skill, may eafily kill an ignorant Giant; fo a fmall Army that hath experienced Commanders, may eafily overcome a great Army that hath none.

L.

That Gallant men having no employment for Heroick Actions, become lazy, as hating any other bufinefs; whereas Cowards and bafe perfons are onely active and ftirring in times of Peace, working ill defigns to breed Factions, and caufe difturbances in a Common-wealth.

LI.

That there have been many Queftions and Difputes concerning the Governments of Princes; as, Whether they ought to govern by Love, or Fear? But the beft way of Government is, and has always been by juft Rewards and Punifhments; for that State which cannot tell how and when to punifh and reward, does not know how to govern, by reafon all the World is governed that way.

LII.

LII.

That if the ancienr *Britains* had had skill, according to their Courage, they might have conquer'd all the World, as the *Romans* did.

LIII.

That it would be very beneficial for great Princes to be sometimes present in Courts of Judicature, to examine the Causes of their poor Subjects, and find out the Extortions and Corruptions of Magistrates and Officers; by which glorious Act they would gain much Love and Fame from the People.

LIV.

That it would be very advantagious for Subjects, and not in the least prejudicial to the Soveraign, to have a general Register in every County, for the Entry of all manner of Deeds, and Conveyance of Land between party and party, and Offices of Record; for by this means, whosoever buyes, would see clearly what Interest and Title there is in any Land he intends to purchase, whereby he shall be assur'd that the Sale made to him is good and firm, and prevent many Law-suits touching the Title of his Purchase.

LV.

That there should be a Limitation for Law-Suits; and that the longest Suit should not last above two Tearms, at length not above a Year; which would certainly be a great benefit to the Subjects in general, though not to Lawyers; and though some Polititi-
ans

ans object, That the more the people is bufie about their private Affairs, the lefs time have they to make difturbanee in the publick; yet this is but a weak Argument, fince Law-fuits are as apt to breed Factions, as any thing elfe; for they bring people into poverty, that they know not how to live, which muft of neceffity breed difcontent, and put them upon ill defigns.

LVI.

That Power, for the moft part, does more then Wifdom; for Fools with Power, feem wife; whereas wife men, without Power, feem Fools; and this is the reafon that the World takes Power for Wifdom; and the want of Power for Foolifhnefs.

LVII.

That a valiant man will not refufe an honourable Duel; nor a wife man fight upon a Fools Quarrel.

LVIII.

That men are apt to find fault with each other's actions; believing they prove themfelves wife in finding fault with their Neighbours.

LIX.

That a wife man will draw feveral occafions to the point of his defign, as a Burning-Glafs doth the feveral beams of the Sun.

LX

LX.

That although actions may be prudently deſigned, and valiantly performcd; yet none can warrant the iſſue; for Fortune is more powerful then Prudence, and had *Cæſar* not been fortunate, his Valour and Prudence would never have gained him ſo much applauſe.

LXI.

That ill Fortune, makes wiſe and honeſt men ſeem Fools and Kanves; but good Fortune makes Fools and Knaves ſeem wiſe and honeſt men.

LXII.

That ill Fortune doth oftner ſucceed good, then good Fortune ſucceeds ill ; for thoſe that have ill Fortune, do not ſo eaſily recover it, as thoſe that have good Fortune are apt to loſe it.

LXIII.

That he had obſerved, That ſeldom any perſon did laugh, but it was at the follies or misfortunes of other men; by which we may judg of their good natures.

LXIV.

I have heard my Lord ſay, That when he was in Baniſhment, He had nothing left him, but a clear Conſcience, by which he had and did ſtill conquer all the Armies of misfortunes that ever ſeized upon him.

LXV.

Alſo I have heard him ſay, That he was never beholding to Lady Fortune; for he had ſuffered on both ſides, although he never was but on one ſide.

Z z   LXVI.

LXVI.

I have heard him say, That his Father one time, upon some discourse of expences, should tell him, *It was but just that every man should have his time.*

LXVII.

I have heard my Lord say, That bold soliciting and intruding men, shall gain more by their importunate Petitions, then modest honest men shall get by silence (as being loath to offend, or be too troublesome) both in the manner and matter of their requests: The reason is, said he, That Great Princes will rather grant sometimes an unreasonable suit, then be tired with frequent Petitions, and hindered from their ordinary Pleasures; And when I asked my Lord, whether the Grants of such importunate suits were fitly and properly placed? He answered, Not so well as those that are placed upon due consideration, and upon trial and proof.

LXVIII.

I have heard my Lord say, That it is a great Error, and weak Policy in a State, to advance their Enemies, and endeavour to make them friends by bribing them with Honours and Offices, saying, They are shrewd men, and may do the State much hurt: And on the other side, to neglect their Friends, and those that have done them great service, saying, they are Honest men, and mean the State no harm: For this kind of Policy comes from the Heathen, who pray'd to the Devil, and not to God, by reason they supposed God was Good,

and

and would hurt no Creature; but the Devil they
flatter'd and worſhipp'd out of fear, leſt he ſhould
hurt them: But by this fooliſh Policy, ſaid he, they
moſt commonly encreaſe their Enemies, and loſe
their Friends; for firſt, it teaches men to obſerve, that
the onely way to Preferment, is to be againſt the State
or Government: Next, Since all that are Factious,
cannot be rewarded or preferr'd, by reaſon a State
hath more Subjects, then Rewards or Preferments,
there muſt of neceſſity be numerous Enemies; for
when their hopes of Reward fail them, they grow
more Factious and Inveterate then ever they were at
firſt: Wherefore the beſt Policy in a State or Government, ſaid my Lord, is to reward Friends, and
puniſh Enemies, and prefer the Honeſt before the Factious; and then all will be real Friends, and profer
their honeſt ſervice, either out of pure Love and
Loyalty, or in hopes of Advancement, ſeeing there
is none but by ſerving the State.

LXIX.

I have heard him ſay ſeveral times, That his love
to his gracious Maſter King *Charles* the Second, was
above the love he bore to his Wife, Children, and
all his Poſterity, nay to his own life: And when,
ſince His Return into *England*, I anſwer'd him, That
I obſerved His Gracious Maſter did not love him ſo
well as he lov'd Him; he replied, That he cared not
whether His Majeſty lov'd him again or not; for he
was reſolved to love him.   LXX

LXX.

I asking my Lord one time, What kind of Fate it was, that reſtored our Gracious King, *Charles* the Second, to His Throne? He anſwer'd, It was a bleſſed kind of Fate. I replied, That I had obſerved a perfect contrariety between the Fortunes of His Royal Father, of bleſſed memory, and Him; for as there was a diviſion amongſt the generality of the people, in the Reign of King *Charles* the Firſt, tending to His Deſtruction; ſo there was a general Combination and Agreement between them in King *Charles* the Second His Reſtauration; and as there was a general malice amongſt the people againſt the Father to Depoſe Him; ſo there was a general Love for the Son to Enthrone Him. My Lord anſwer'd, I had obſerved ſomething, but not all; for, ſaid he, there was a Neceſſity for the people to deſire and Reſtore King *Charles* the Second; but there was no Neceſſity to Murder King *Charles* the Firſt. For the Kingdom being through ſo many Alterations and Changes of Government, divided into ſeveral Factions and Parties, was at laſt hurried into ſuch a Confuſion, that it was impoſſible in that manner to ſubſiſt, or hold out any longer; Which Confuſion having opened the Peoples Eyes, the generality being tyred with the evil effects and conſequences of their unſetled Governments under unjuſt Uſurpers, and frightned with the apprehenſion of future dangers, began to call to

mind

mind the happy Times, when in an uninterrupted
Peace they enjoyed their own, under the happy
Reign of their Lawful Soveraigns; and hereupon
with an unanimous consent Recall'd and Restor'd our
now gracious King; which, although it was opposed
by some Factious Parties, yet the generality of the
people outweigh'd the rest; neither was the Royal Party wanting in their endeavours.

LXXI.

Asking my Lord one time, Whether it was easie
or difficult to govern a State or Kingdom? He answer'd me, That most States were govern'd by secret
Policy, and so with difficulty; for those that govern,
are (at least, should be) wiser then the State or Commonwealth they govern. I replied, That in my opinion, a State was easily govern'd, if their Government was like unto God's; that is to say, If Governours did Reward and Punish according to the desert.
My Lord answer'd, I said well; but he added, the
Follies of the People are many times too hard for the
Prudence of the Governour; like as the sins of men
work more evil effects in them, then the Grace of
God works good; for if this were not, there would
be more good then bad, which, alas, Experience proves
otherwise.

LXXII.

Some Gentlemen making a complaint to my Lord,
That some he employed in His Majesty's Affairs, were

too

too hafty and over-bufie. My Lord told them, That
he would rather chufe fuch perfons for His Majefties
fervice as were over-active, then fuch that would be
fuller of Queftions then Actions. The fame he would
do for his own particular affairs.

LXXIII.

Some condemning My Lord for having *Roman-
Catholicks* and *Scots* in his Army; He anfwered them, that
he did not examine their Opinions in Religion, but
look'd more upon their Honefty and Duty ; for certainly there were honeft men and loyal Subjects a-
mongft *Roman Catholicks*, as well as Proteftants ; and
amongft *Scots* as well as *Englifh*. Neverthelefs, my
Lord, as he was for the King, fo he was alfo for the
Orthodox Church of *England*, as fufficiently appears
by the care he took in ordering the Church-Govern-
ment, mentioned in the Hiftory. To which purpofe,
when my Lord was walking one time with fome of His
Officers in the Church at *Durham*, and wonder'd at
the greatnefs and ftrength of the Pillars that fupported
that ftructure ; My Brother, Sir *Charles Lucas*, who
was then with him, told my Lord, that he muft con-
fefs, thofe Pillars were very great, and of a vaft ftrength;
But faid he, Your Lordfhip is a far greater Pillar of
the Church then all thefe : Which certainly was alfo
a real truth, and would have more evidently appear'd,
had Fortune favour'd my Lord more then fhe did.

LXXIV. My

LXXIV.

My Lord being in Banishment, I told him, that he was happy in his misfortunes, for he was not subject to any State or Prince. To which he jestingly answer'd, That as he was subject to no Prince, so he was a Prince of no Subjects.

LXXV.

In some Discourse which I had with my Lord concerning Princes and their Sujects; I declared that I had observed Great Princes were not like the Sun, which sends forth out of it self Rays of Light, and Beams of Heat; effects that did both glorifie the Sun, and nourish and comfort sublunary Creatures; but their glory and splendor proceeded rather from the Ceremony which they received from their subjects. To which my Lord answer'd, That Subjects were so far from giving splendor to their Princes, that all the Honours and Titles, in which consists the chief splendor of a subject, were principally derived from them; for, said he, were there no Princes, there would be none to confer Honours and Titles upon them.

LXXVI.

My Lord entertaining one time some Gentlemen with a merry Discourse, told them, that he would not keep them Company except they had done and sufferd as much for their King and Country as he had. They answer'd, That they had not a power answerable to my Lords. My Lord replied, They should do

their

their endeavour according to their Abilities : No, said they, if we did, we should be like your Self, lose all, and get but little for our pains.

LXXVII.

I being much grieved that my Lord for his loyalty and honest Service, had so many Enemies, used sometimes to speak somewhat sharply of them; but he gently reproving me, said, *I should do like experienced Sea-men, and as they either turn their Sails with the wind, or take them down; so should I either comply with Time, or abate my Passion.*

LXXVIII.

A Soldiers Wife, whose Husband had been slain in my Lord's Army, came one time to beg some relief of my Lord; who told her, That he was not able to relieve all that had been loyal to His Majesty ; for said he, My losses are so many, that if I should give away the remainder of my Estate, my Wife and Children would have nothing to live on: She answer'd, That His Majesty's Enemies were preferr'd to great Honours, and had much Wealth : Then it is a sign (replied my Lord) that your Husband and I were Honest Men.

LXXIX.

A Friend of my Lord's, complaining that he had done the State much Service, but received little Reward for it; my Lord answer'd him, That States did not usually reward past Services; but if he could do
some

fome prefent Service, he might perhaps get fomething; but (faid he) thofe men are wifeft that will be paid before-hand.

LXXX.

I obferving that in the late Civil Warrs, many were defirous to be employed in States Affairs, and at the noife of Warr, endeavoured to be Commanders, though but of fmall Parties, asked my Lord the reafon thereof, and what advantage they could make by their Employments? My Lord fmilingly anfwer'd, That for the generality, he knew not what they could get, but danger, lofs and labour for their pains. Then I ask'd him, Whether Generals of Great Armies were ever enriched by their Heroick Exploits, and great Victories? My Lord anfwer'd, That ordinary Commanders gained more, and were better rewarded then great Generals. To which I added, That I had obferv'd the fame in Hiftories, namely, That men of great Merit and Power, had not onely no Rewards, but were either found fault withall, or laid afide when they had no more bufinefs or employment for them; and that I could not conceive any reafon for it, but that States were afraid of their Power: My Lord anfwer'd, The reafon was, That it was far more eafie to reward Under-Officers, then Great Commanders.

Bbb   LXXXI.

LXXXI.

My Lord having since the Return from his Banishment, set up a Race of Horses, instead of those he lost by the Warrs, uses often to ride through his Park to see his Breed. One time it chanced when he went thorough it, that he espied some labouring-men sawing of Woods that were blown down by the Wind, for some particular uses; at which my Lord turning to his Attendants, said, That he had been at that Work a great part of his life. They not knowing what my Lord meant, but thinking he jested; I speak very seriously, (added he) and not in jest; for you see that this Tree which is blown down by the Wind, although it was sound and strong, yet it could not withstand its force; and now it is down, it must be cut in pieces, and made serviceable for several uses; whereof some will serve for Building, some for Paling, some for Firing, &c. In the like manner, said he, have I been cut down by the Lady Fortune; and being not able to resist so Powerful a Princess, I have been forced to make the best use of my Misfortunes, as the Chips of my Estate.

LXXXII.

My Lord discoursing one time with some of his Friends, of judging of other mens Natures, Dispositions and Actions; and some observing that men could not possibly know or judg of them, the events of mens actions falling out oftentimes contrary to their

inten-

intentions ; fo that where they hit once, they fail'd
twenty times in their Judgments. My Lord anfwer'd,
That his Judgment in that point feldom did mifs, although he thought it weaker then theirs : The reafon
is, faid he, Becaufe I judg moft men to be like my felf ;
that is to fay, Fools ; when as you do judg them all
according to your felf, that is, Wife men ; and fince
there are more Fools in the World then Wife men, I
may fooner guefs right then you : for though my judgment roves at random, yet it can never mifs of Errors ;
which yours will never do, except you can dive into
other mens Follies by the length of your own line, and
found their bottom by the weight of your own Plum-
met, for the depth of Folly is beyond the line of
Wifdom.

Befides, faid he, You believe that other men would
do as you would have them, or as you would do to
them ; wherein you are miftaken, for moft men do
the contrary. In fhort, Folly is bottomlefs, and hath
no end ; but Wifdom hath bounds to all her defigns,
otherwife fhe would never compafs them.

LXXXIII.

My Lord difcourfing fome time with a Learned
Doctor of Divinity concerning Faith, faid, That in
his opinion, the wifeft way for a man, was to have as
little Faith as he could for this World, and as much as
he could for the next World.

LXXXIV.

LXXXIV.

In some Discourse with my Lord, I told him that I did speak sharpest to those I loved best. To which he jestingly answered, That if so, then he would not have me love him best.

LXXXV.

After my Lords return from a long Banishment, when he had been in the Countrey some time, and endeavoured to pick up some Gleanings of his ruined Estate; it chanced that the Widow of *Charles* Lord *Mansfield,* My Lords Eldest Son, afterwards Duchess of *Richmond,* to whom the said Lord of *Mansfield* had made a joynture of 2000 l. a Year, died not long after her second marriage; for whose death, though My Lord was heartily sorry, and would willingly have lost the said Money, had it been able to save her life; Yet discoursing one time merrily with his Friends, was pleased to say, That though his Earthly King and Master seem'd to have forgot him, yet the King of Heaven had remembred him, for he had given him 2000 l. a Year.

SOME

SOME FEW
NOTES
OF THE
AUTHORESSE.

I.

IT was far more difficult in the late Civil Wars, for my Lord to raife an Army for His Majefties Service, then it was for the Parliament to raife an Army againft His Majefty: Not onely becaufe the Parliament were many, and my Lord but one fingle Perfon; but by reafon a Kingly or Monarchical Government was then generally difliked, and moft part of the Kingdom proved Rebellious, and affifted the Parliament either with their Purfes or Perfons, or both; when as the Army which my Lord raifed for the defence and maintenance of the King, and his Rights, was raifed moft upon his own and his Friends Intereft: For it is frequently feen and known by woful Experience, that rebellious and factious Parties do more fuddenly and nnmeroufly flock together to act a mifchievous defign,

then

then loyal and honeſt men to aſſiſt or maintain a juſt
Cauſe; and certainly 'tis much to be lamented, that
evil men ſhould be more induſtrious and proſperous
then good, and that the Wicked ſhould have a more
deſperate Courage, then the Virtuous, an active Valour.

II.

I have obſerved, That many by flattering Poets,
have been compared to *Cæſar*, without deſert; but this
I dare freely and without flattery ſay of my Lord,
That though he had not *Cæſars* Fortune, yet he wanted not *Cæſars* Courage, nor his Prudence, nor his
good Nature, nor his Wit; Nay, in ſome particulars
he did more then *Cæſar* ever did; for though *Cæſar*
had a great Army, yet he was firſt ſet ont by the State
or Senators of *Rome*, who were Maſters almoſt of all
the World; when as my Lord raiſed his Army (as before is mentioned) moſt upon his own Intereſt (he
having many Friends and Kindred in the Northern
parts) at ſuch a time when his Gracious King and Soveraign was then not Maſter of his own Kingdoms, He
being over-power'd by his rebellious Subjects.

III.

I have obſerved, That my Noble Lord has always
                                                    had

had an averfion to that kind of Policy, that now is commonly practifed in the world, which in plain tearms is Diffembling, Flattery and Cheating, under the cover of Honefty, Love and Kindnefs: But I have heard him fay, that the beft Policy is to act juftly, honeftly and wifely, and to fpeak truly; and that the old Proverb is true; *To be wife is to be honeft:* For, faid he, That man of what Condition, Quality or Profeffion foever, that is once found out to deceive either in words or actions, fhall never be trufted again by wife and honeft men. But, faid he, A wife man is not bound to take notice of all Diffemblers, and their cheating Actions, if they do not concern him; nay, even of thofe he would not always take notice, but chufe his time; for the chief part of a wife man is to time bufinefs well, and to do it without Partiality and Paffion. But, faid he, The folly of the world is fo great, that one honeft and wife man may be overpowred by many Knaves and Fools; and if fo, then the onely benefit of a wife man confifts in the fatisfaction he finds by his honeft and wife actions, and that he has done what in Confcience, Honour and Duty he ought to do; and all fucceffors of fuch worthy Perfons ought to be more fatisfied in the worth and merit of their Predeceffours, then in their Title and Riches.

I have heard that some noble Gentleman, (who was servant to His Highness then Prince of *Wales*, our now Gracious Soveraign, when my Lord was Governour) should relate, that whensoever my Lord by his prudent inspection and foresight did foretell what would come to pass hereafter; it seemed so improbable to him, that both himself and some others believed my Lord spoke extravagantly: But some few years after, his predictions proved true, and the event did confirm what his Prudence had observed.

V.

I have heard, That in our late Civil Warres there were many petty Skirmishes, and Fortifications of weak and inconsiderable Houses, where some small Parties would be shooting and pottering at each other; an action more proper for Bandites or Thieves, then stout and valiant Soldiers; for I have heard my Lord say, That such small Parties divide the Body of an Army, and by that means weaken it; whereas the business might be much easier decided in one or two Battels, with less ruine both to the Country and Army: For I have heard my Lord say, That as it is dangerous to divide a Limb from the Body; so it is also

dan-

dangerous to divide Armies or Navies in time of
Warr; and there are often more men loft in fuch petty Skirmifhes, then in fet-Battels, by reafon thofe
happen almoft every day, nay every hour in feveral
places.

VI.

Many in our late Civil-Warres, had more Title
then Power; for though they were Generals, or chief
Commanders, yet their Forces were more like a Bri-
gade, then a well-formed Army; and their actions were
accordingly, not fet-battels, but petty Skirmifhes between fmall Parties; for there were no great Battels
fought, but by my Lord's Army, his being the greateft and beft-formed Army which His Majefty had.

VII.

Although I have obferved, That it is a ufual Cu-
ftom of the World, to glorifie the prefent Power
and good Fortune, and vilifie ill Fortune and low
conditions; yet I never heard that my Noble Lord
was ever neglected by the generality; but was on the
contrary, alwayes efteemed and praifed by all;
for he is truly an Honeft and Honourable man, and
one that may be relied upon both for Truft and
Truth.

VIII.

VIII.

I have obferved, That many inftead of great. A-
ctions, make onely a great Noife; and like fhallow
Fords, or empty Bladders, found moft when there is
leaft in them; which expreffes a flattering Partiality,
rather then Honefty and Truth; for Truth and Honefty lye at the bottom, and have more Action then
Shew.

IX.

I have obferved, That good Fortune adds Fame
to mean Actions, when as ill Fortune darkens the
fplendor of the moft meritorious; for mean Perfons
plyed with good Fortune, are more famous then Noble Perfons that are fhadowed or darkned with ill
Fortune; fo that Fortune, for the moft part, is Fame's
Champion.

X.

I obferve, That as it would be a grief to covetous
and miferable perfons, to be rewarded with Honour,
rather then with Wealth, becaufe they love Wealth,
before Honour and Fame; fo on the other fide, Noble, Heroick and Meritorious Perfons, prefer Honour
and Fame before Wealth; well knowing, That as In-
famy

famy is the greatest Punishment of unworthiness, so
Fame and Honour is the best Reward of worth and
merit.

XII.

I observe, that spleen and malice, especially in this
age, is grown to that height, that none will endure
the praise of any body besides themselves ; nay, they'l
rather praise the wicked then the good ; the Coward
rather then the Valiant ; the Miserable then the Generous ; the Traytor, then the Loyal : which makes
Wise men meddle as little with the Affairs of the
world as ever they can.

XIII.

I have observed, as well as former Ages have done,
That Meritorious persons, for their noble actions, most
commonly get Envy and Reproach, instead of Praise
and Reward ; unless their Fortunes be above Envy,
as *Cæsars* and *Elexanders* were ; But had these two
Worthies been as Unfortunate as they were Fortunate, they would have been as much vilified, as they
are glorified.

XIV.

I have observed, that it is more easie to talk, then to
act ; to forget, then to remember ; to punish, then to

reward; and more common to prefer Flattery before
Truth, Intereſt before Juſtice, and preſent ſervice before paſt.

XV.

I have obſerved, that many old Proverbs are very
true, and amongſt the reſt, this : It is better to be at
the latter end of a Feaſt, then at the beginning of a Fray;
for moſt commonly, thoſe that are in the beginning of
a Fray, get but little of the Feaſt; and thoſe that have
undergone the greateſt dangers, have leaſt of the
ſpoils.

XVI.

I have oberved, That Favours of Great Princes
make men often thought Meritorious; whereas without them, they would be eſteemed but as ordinary Perſons.

XVII.

I obſerve, That in other Kingdoms or Countries, to
be the chief Governour of a Province, is not onely
a place of Honour, but much Profit ; for they have a
great Revenue to themſelves; whereas in *England*, the
Lieutenancy of a County is barely a Title of Honour,
without Profit ; except it be the Lieutenancy or Government of the Kingdom of *Ireland* ; eſpecially ſince
the late Earl of *Stafford* enjoyed that dignity, who
                                                                    ſetled

ſetled that Kingdom very wiſely both for Militia and Trade.

XVIII.

I have obſerved, That thoſe that meddle leaſt in Wars, whether Civil or Foreign, are not onely moſt ſafe and free from danger, but moſt ſecure from Loſſes; and though Heroick Perſons eſteem Fame before Life; yet many there are, that think the wiſeſt way is to be a Spectator, rather then an Actor, unleſs they be neceſſitated to it ; for it is better, ſay they, to ſit on the Stool of Quiet , then in the Chair of Troubleſome Buſineſs.

F I N I S.

www.ingramcontent.com/pod-product-compliance
Lightning Source LLC
Chambersburg PA
CBHW030319270326
41926CB00010B/1434